Make Your Quilting Pay for Itself

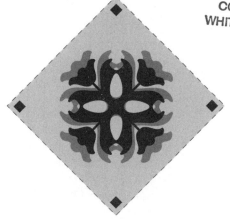

SYLVIA ANN LANDMAN

BETTERWAY BOOKS
CINCINNATI, OHIO

Other fine Betterway Books are available from your local bookstore or direct from the publisher.

01   00   99   98   97   5   4   3   2   1

Library of Congress Cataloging-in-Publication Data

Landman, Sylvia
    Make your quilting pay for itself / Sylvia Ann Landman.
        p.   cm.
   Includes index.
   ISBN 1-55870-446-9 (alk. paper)
   1. Needlework industry and trade. 2. Handicraft industries. 3. Home-based businesses. 4. Quilting—Economic aspects. I. Title.
HD9936.5.A2L36   1997
746.46′ 068—dc21   97-23573
                                                  CIP

Edited by Diana Martin
Production edited by Michelle Kramer
Interior designed by Kathleen DeZarn
Cover designed by Cathleen Shaw/Copperleaf Design
Cover photography by Pam Monfort Braun/Bronze Photography
Cover quilt by Sylvia Ann Landman

Nine very special quilters profiled in this book richly deserve this dedication. They answered my questions and endured my probing into their personal histories and quilting endeavors. They willingly spent valuable time reaching out to unknown readers of this book to educate, motivate and inspire.

Without their valuable contributions, this book would be undernourished and incomplete. For your patience and generous sharing so that others may learn, I thank you one and all:

Millie Becker

Margie Bevis

Karen Brown

Karen Combs

Mary and Ozz Graham

Daphne Greig

Julie Higgins

Morna McEver Golletz

Barbara Barrick McKie

About the Author

PHOTO BY MORGAN J. COWIN

Sylvia Ann Landman began her career in fiber arts in 1960 doing dressmaking, custom knitting, crochet and embroidery from a home studio. Not long afterward, it became a teaching studio as well.

She began teaching classes in needlework and fiber arts for California Community Colleges in 1962. Students from these classes were increasingly curious as to how Sylvia made her livelihood in the creative arts.

Sylvia's response was to add business and entrepreneurial classes to her teaching schedule to show them they could do it too! Two of her most popular classes today are Your Arts in the Marketplace and How to Start a Mail-Order Business.

Today, she is involved in fiber arts full time, in addition to writing about the business end of crafts for many craft and other publications. She is the author of *Crafting for Dollars, Turn Your Hobby Into Serious Cash* (Prima Publishing, 1996). Magazines regularly publish her original needlework and quilting designs. She writes a regular column for *Lady's Circle Patchwork Quilts*. The Knitting Guild of America invited her to design and teach a class by correspondence for their guild members nationwide. Both she and her students found the experience rewarding.

Recently, she traveled to England and Scotland with the Rowan Wool tours. While there, she interviewed internationally known author/designers including Kaffe Fassett, Sasha Kagan and the curator of the Fair-Isle Knitting Museum in the Shetland Islands.

Sylvia still teaches weekly classes at her home studio and for local community colleges. She travels extensively throughout the U.S. giving workshops and lectures at regional and national seminars.

Table of Contents

Foreword

My first encounter with Sylvia Landman was at a national seminar of the members of the Society of Craft Designers. She was lecturing to a group of crafting professionals on the subject of marketing your creativity. These were people who made a living out of their craft, and they gave Sylvia their undivided attention for one very good reason—she knew what she was talking about.

It was this introduction to Sylvia that inspired me to trust her to write knowledgeable, thorough and informative articles for three magazines I have edited. She has a way of imparting information in a manner that is easy to understand, and clears up confusing issues that can be daunting to crafters, quilters, needleworkers and other small business people. The nuances of marketing, sales and channeling the creative spirit are addressed and made accessible in her writing.

Sylvia's knowledge and insight into the business of crafting is evidenced by the fact that she successfully markets her own quilting and needlework. She has turned a cottage business into a profitable enterprise, is very visible in the industry and has made her name synonymous with efficient, quality work.

Now she is sharing her insights with others who wish to use their talents and determination to break into the world of professional quiltmaking and designing. The message is clear: Whether you want to make quilts to sell, market patterns, represent product manufacturers or write about your work, you can make your quilting pay for itself—if you have the know-how.

Terri Nyman
Editor, Lady's Circle Patchwork Quilts *and* Quilt Craft
Former editor, Creative Product News

Introduction

Do you hope to earn a few extra dollars with your quilting skills? If so, there is plenty of room for you in today's quilting industry, valued at $1,554 billion and still rising! Let's take a closer look at the size of this industry in the U.S.

- The Hobby Industry Association's 1994 Nationwide Consumer Craft Study found that 90 percent of U.S. households have at least one family member engaged in craft hobbies, which includes quilting. This figure is up from 82 percent in 1992 and 77 percent in 1990. What will the 1996 survey bring?

- In 1994, *Quilter's Newsletter Magazine* and the International Quilt Market/Festival in Houston commissioned the first exclusive survey of the U.S. quilting market. The First National Survey ™ of Quilting in America found that 14.7 percent (14,091,000) of American homes house a quilter.

According to this survey, these quilters were expected to spend $476 million on tools and supplies plus a staggering $353 million on fabric in 1996! Figures like these erase the notion that quilting is a frivolous pastime.

Karoline (Karey) Bresenhan, successful Houston quilt shop owner, anticipated a phenomenal growth in the quilting industry as early as 1970. With many supporters, she founded two organizations to help the movement expand. The International Quilt Market serves quilting professionals, shop owners, teachers, designers and writers. Following the Market, the International Quilt Festival began. The Festival serves quilt hobbyists and offers classes, lectures and special exhibits. Each fall, both shows, which are held in Houston, draw up to 51,000 quilters from all over the world (yes, *world*). Quilters from twenty-five foreign countries join American enthusiasts to participate in classes, lectures and seminars, and to view hundreds of quilts and dozens of special exhibits.

The International Quilt Market is the only wholesale trade show in the world exclusively supporting the quilting and soft crafts industry. Retailers from across the nation set up more than five hundred merchant booths in the 250,000 square foot exhibit hall at the George R. Brown Convention Center each fall. Together, the retail and wholesale shows create a vital catalyst, enabling the quilting industry to continue to grow.

The Insider, a publication of Quilts, Inc., parent company of the International Quilt Market, announced in its Summer 1996 issue that attendance exceeded the three thousand mark at the 1996 Spring edition of the International Quilt Market in Portland, Oregon. The quilting industry's trade show attracted a total of 3,186 people compared to the 1995 event, which drew 2,300 registrants. The Portland Market also drew a record number of international buyers.

Karen Ancona, editor of the trade publication, *Craft & Needlework Age,* writes in the April 1996 issue, "Unquestionably, quilting as a hobby for mainstream America (and, in fact, the world) has been nourished by two factors: the fine work of Karey Bresenhan, and the proliferation of quilting books. We credit Karey with founding and focusing an industry, while we must credit books about quilts with enlisting and educating a growing number of admirers and artisans."

Other Quilt-Related Activities

The popularity of quilting has also spawned quilt-related activities such as:
- Televised programs on the Public Broadcasting System devoted to quilting
- Worldwide quilting conferences, symposiums, workshops, guilds and markets
- Affiliated organizations such as the Alliance for American Quilts, an umbrella group that strives to unite elements of the quilt world and to establish quilting as an art form
- The American International Quilt Association, dedicated to preserving the art of quilting throughout the world
- Publishers who specialize in publishing quilting books
- Quilting websites on the World Wide Web
- Numerous quilting electronic chat and news groups for hobbyists and professionals
- Quilt museums
- The Quilter's Hall of Fame
- Quilt exhibits in prestigious museums throughout the world
- Fashion shows such as the well-known traveling Fairfield Wearable Art Show, which incorporates quilting techniques into wearing apparel

About Today's Quilters

Who are all these quilters? What do they want? How do quilters remain so motivated? What do they do with all those quilts? The First National Survey ™ of Quilting in

America provides additional answers to several of these questions.

Dedicated quilters are defined as possessing intermediate to advanced skills, averaging 10.5 years of experience and quilting 40.2 hours monthly. They complete an average of 12.7 new projects annually. Their average age is 52, though 32 percent are between 18 and 44.

The average quilter owns $922 worth of fabric and $2,572 worth of other quilting supplies. Thirty percent of quilters reported that they own even more than this! Most quilters are women, but not exclusively. Many talented men contribute to the quilt movement as authors, teachers, designers and manufacturers of important equipment such as quilting frames, measuring devices and template materials.

Today's quilters want to express their creativity through quilting. Classes taught by nationally known teachers, artists and experts frequently overflow with quilters demanding to learn new techniques. They want to know more about color and design in order to create innovative art quilts. They also want to know more about the historical aspects tied so closely to American quilting. Particular groups dedicate themselves to exploring colonial America by identifying fabrics, style, color and messages found in early quilts. Classes and seminars exist to teach quilters to appraise quilts and to restore the quilted treasures from past centuries.

Motivation and a thirst for increased skills drive quilters to want more. Manufacturers rush to fill the demand with an increasing array of fabrics and better tools, such as rotary cutters to replace scissors and specially designed quilters' rulers in place of measuring tapes.

Today, quilters do not stop at making bed coverings. Modern-day quilters make wall hangings of all dimensions, table coverings, pillows, framed pictures (sometimes even including a quilted frame), clothing accessories of all types and a myriad of small specialty items such as pincushions, place mats and even specially designed cases to carry—what else?—quilts in progress.

Quilting as an Addiction

Quilting often becomes addictive! Serious quilters describe their symptoms regularly in newsletters, magazines and chat groups on the Internet. Here are some of the most common:

- I can't stop buying fabric even though I have so much. My sewing room is bulging.
- I must stop all other activities when quilting magazines I subscribe to arrive. I read them cover to cover before resuming household or career tasks.

- So many quilting classes and workshops beckon to me. Should I attend them all? How will I know when I've taken enough classes?
- There are many chat groups devoted to quilting topics on the Internet. Reading every message takes several hours, but I am afraid I will miss something unless I read them all. Do others have this problem?
- While vacationing, I feel compelled to go from one quilt shop to another. I've sent for the list of shops throughout the country recommended by others who also combine out-of-state vacations with quilt shop visits. How much time should I spend on this without ruining a trip for my entire family?

Solutions and suggestions abound to help quilt addicts channel their passion in positive directions.

Magazines and newsletters written for quilters continually address the undisputed characteristic of a quilt addict: fabric codependency. Quilt addicts write to magazines and chat groups asking questions like these:

- "How should I sort my fabric collection—by color or print?"
- "How much fabric should I buy when I have no immediate use for it, but *must* have it?"
- "My car's trunk, closets and under-the-bed space are full of fabric. Where do others store their fabric (known in quilter's jargon as 'fabric-stash')?"
- "Which electronic sewing machine should I buy for machine quilting?"
- "I make quilt tops faster than I can hand-quilt them. Can anyone recommend someone who will finish them for me so I can keep making more?"

Articles about selecting, purchasing, storing and managing equipment, tools, books and patterns are the mainstays of quilting publications. Recently, one of the magazines devoted to quilters even offered tips about how to travel by air hand-carrying one's sewing machine and supplies to quilt markets and conferences.

As a quilting addict myself, my own foray into the quilting world includes:

- Covering all my beds and walls with quilts
- Teaching quilting, certified by the National Quilting Association
- Writing about quilting as a freelancer and columnist for several magazines
- Selling original quilt designs to both quilting and craft publications
- Lecturing to college classes about how to turn craft skills into profit
- And most importantly, I, too, quilt to create, use my fabric stash, have fun and relax

Most quilt enthusiasts have several characteristics in common. Use the questions listed below, to determine which ones describe you.

- Are you a quilt fabric addict?
- Do you use modern quilting techniques such as rotary cutters and invisible thread?
- Have you given quilts and related items as gifts to everyone you know?
- Have you learned to machine quilt so you can make more quilts faster?
- Have you covered your beds and walls with quilts of all sizes?
- Do you search for justification to continue buying quilting supplies and making quilts?
- Do you feel guilty as you spend even more money to support your quilting habit?
- Do you want to become a part of the worldwide quilting industry?
- Have you asked yourself the question, "Is it possible to make extra money from quilting?"

If you answered the last question with a resounding "Yes," this book will help you. You will find tips, ideas and step-by-step procedures to help you *Make Your Quilting Pay for Itself*.

GETTING READY

Converting your quilting hobby into a small profit-making venture requires preparation, which begins by taking inventory. But before you check your quilting supplies or your bank account, examine your most valuable asset—yourself!

Characteristics You Should Have

Working where you live, even part time, becomes easier if you have or can develop a few special personality characteristics. According to the Small Business Administration (SBA), certain personality traits contribute more to success in business than the amount of money you have to invest.

Self-motivation heads the list of desirable personality traits. Self-motivation means the ability to work on your own at specific chores without anyone prodding you to get started or to keep working. You have the drive to keep yourself moving forward. Does this describe you?

Reliability comes next. When you promise to complete a project by a certain date, how's your track record? Can others depend on you? When you set goals, make appointments or set a work schedule for yourself, how do you rate? If you see yourself as self-motivated, prompt, conscientious and well organized, your chances to profit from your quiltmaking skills rank high.

Does procrastination derail your reliability? Like Scarlett O'Hara, do you put off until tomorrow what you should do today? Do you only work when you feel like it? Do you often misplace things only to find yourself searching for something you need but cannot find? If this describes you, step back and reconsider. Though procrastination may not disrupt your personal life, it contributes to the downfall of many entrepreneurs—part-time or full-time.

The ability to cope is a must. If you hope to profit from your quilting skills, your customers, students and clients must be able to depend on you. How well do you come through in a pinch? If a time crunch occurs, how well do you cope? Successful entrepreneurs have contingency plans. They prepare for the unexpected and have a plan of action ready when it happens. Do you?

The ability to prioritize is critical. Do you generally meet your deadlines? If you promise a finished quilt to a customer by the first of next month, do you stand behind your word? Meeting deadlines must take precedence over mundane matters such as organizing your fabric or designing your next project. If you develop the ability to rank tasks and deadlines in order of importance, you have won half the battle when working from home.

Setting a Work Schedule and Sticking to It

Managing a home while conducting an efficient business challenges everyone. Doing so when you *work* where you *live* magnifies that challenge. Distractions wait around every corner. Telephones, doorbells, pets and neighbors may search you out saying, "But you're home anyway." Frequent interruptions from small children and other housemates can undo even the most organized work schedule. Thus, the secret to success of home-based crafters is to keep professional and personal worlds organized and well managed but separate.

Here is a method you can try to help you set up a work schedule and stick to it:
1. Divide a sheet of paper in half vertically.
2. List household and personal tasks on the left side of the paper in any order.
3. List quilting and professional chores on the right side.
4. Maintain the lists for a week until every activity that takes your time appears on one side or the other. Call this your first draft.
5. Next, divide another sheet of paper in half. Using your first draft, copy each household activity to the left side of the second draft in order of importance. Place the "must do's" at the top. Continue adding tasks, ending with the mundane, least-demanding jobs at the bottom.

This list should account for every task, ranked in a sensible order. Repeat this process for your quilting and professional chores on the other side of the paper. You have before you a weekly schedule of tasks. Begin each day by tackling the chores that head each side of the lists.

Working with only one week at a time keeps the lists manageable. Check frequently to see if you are on schedule. If too many chores remain undone at the end of the week, either your list was unrealistically long, you became waylaid or you worked too slowly. Try eliminating the least important task from the bottom of each side and prepare a new work schedule for the following week.

Learn to study your work schedule week by week. Do you meet your deadlines?

Do you spend too much time on trivialities? Do you think of yourself as a procrastinator? If you find yourself behind schedule, consider letting go of something less important in favor of a highly profitable task or one that moves your business forward.

Distribute both personal and professional chores evenly throughout the week to avoid burnout. Balance slow, tedious tasks with those requiring more energy. Alternate sitting and standing jobs, and you may find you can work longer without tiring. Always keep your eye on your schedule, making sure you do "first things first."

Continue to modify your work schedule until it suits your personality, work style and responsibilities. Sooner or later, you will find the perfect schedule that will become a regular routine. The purpose of all this is to become the best worker you can possibly be for your favorite employer—yourself!

Defining and Achieving Your Goals

Why is earning money from quilting important to you? Do you want to contribute to your household income or start a savings account? Maybe you just want to buy a new sewing machine or computer. Perhaps you just want your own pin money to buy unlimited quilting supplies.

Finding answers to these questions will help you define your long-term goals. If you don't know how much you want to earn or what an opportunity means to you, you may not become motivated enough to do your best.

List your goals, being as specific as possible. Here are a few examples:

- You want to earn $3,000 to buy a new electronic sewing machine.
- You want to earn enough to buy all of the fabric and books you want.
- You want to earn enough to pay all of your expenses to a major quilting seminar each year.

Once you've defined your goals and are committed to them, post your goal list alongside your work schedule where you can regularly check your progress. Each time you complete a goal, acknowledge it. Put a star beside it on your list or mark it with a highlighter pen.

Create incentives (other than food) to keep yourself moving forward. Buy a piece of equipment you've been wanting or take the time to read a new quilting book. Give yourself a pat on the back so your subconscious mind feels acknowledged. After all, you do not have an employer to praise you. As a self-employed person, you must reward yourself.

Do some goals remain elusive? If so, avoid negative thinking. Determine the reason they're elusive. If the goal was too ambitious, simplify it. If you lacked motivation, ask yourself why. What got in your way? How can you improve next week?

Consider your body rhythms too. Do you perform your best work early in the morning or late in the afternoon? Never work at ordinary tasks during your body's prime energy level or work on something important when your energy is low.

Some people prefer to work all day on their business two or three days a week and attend to personal or household tasks on the remaining days. Others work on business tasks until lunchtime and tend to home-related jobs during the afternoons. Still others work at their business all week and save household responsibilities for the weekends. Choose the style that suits you, your energy level and your family obligations.

The important issues are to create a manageable work schedule, to prioritize your activities and to prevent yourself from becoming waylaid too often. If this concept sounds as if it takes discipline, you are correct. Managing your life, home and small quiltmaking business must be taken seriously if you wish to succeed.

From Sewing Area to Studio

Home-based workers already face the challenge of separating their personal lives from professional tasks. Separate living areas from your work space if at all possible. A studio is a creative environment where artisans design and work at their craft. Referring to *your* space as the "studio" may become the first step in giving it the respect it deserves. You can easily and inexpensively transform your sewing/quilting area into a comfortable, organized studio.

Defining Your Studio Space

Converting a spare bedroom to a studio or sewing room is ideal. After all, it's already heated, cooled and ventilated like the rest of your home. Bathrooms and closet storage are already nearby. "Studio?" you say. "I only have a tiny corner to sew, quilt and store supplies, and it's always a mess! I can never find anything!"

Even if you do not have an entire room to spare, you can convert a portion of a room and identify your new "studio" in simple ways. Divide a bedroom by lining up bookcases in the middle of it. Work on one side, live in the other. Consider a beaded curtain, planter or room divider to separate the living room from your studio. One quilter I know placed a lovely, hand-painted folding screen in the middle of her largest room. Everything from one side of the screen to the windows she considers as the "sewing studio." Living room furniture on the other side of the screen clearly identifies comfortable living quarters.

Gather all of your sewing equipment, tools, fabrics and notions in your studio. If you plan to combine your studio with an office, you may add business items such as a desk, filing cabinet, computer or typewriter, bookcases, phones and a fax machine. The idea is to designate a specific area that means business. In fact, IRS regulations clearly require a "designated work area" if you take the home office deduction. (More about this valuable deduction in chapter five.)

WORK TABLES

Consider a work surface for cutting and laying out patterns and fabric next. How about an older dining room or kitchen table if space allows? Try to position it so you can work, cut and lay out patterns and fabrics from at least three sides.

If your space is too small to leave a work table set up permanently, consider special collapsible, cardboard cutting tables. Use them to lay out, cut or baste quilts in progress. These special tables found at quilt shows and markets fold up and tuck under beds or behind doors when not in use. You can use folding card tables or camping tables in the same way.

EXPAND YOUR SEWING SURFACE

Most of us need more work space around a sewing machine than a sewing machine table model offers. To solve this problem, I bought an old army desk, painted it and covered the top surface with peel-off, adhesive vinyl floor tiles. My husband cut an opening over the center knee well of the desk so the base of the machine sits flush with the surface of the new desktop. This permits easier machine quilting and/ or sewing on large projects. As an extra bonus, I discovered that the shallow middle drawer over the knee well—meant for pencils and small office items—still opened beneath the sewing machine base. It is exactly the right depth to store spools of thread.

One side of the desk contains three large drawers filled with clean, pressed fabric. The other side has several shallow drawers containing countless notions, quilters' rulers, tools, patterns and templates.

The two sliding boards or leaves beside the center drawer have become my quilting friends. Secretaries used them to hold typewriters. I pull mine out to create an L-shaped space around the machine to support a quilt while binding, for example. The added work surface supports the weight of the quilt and keeps it from dragging as it glides through the presser foot.

STORAGE SPACE

A thought about desk drawers. Don't just toss notions into them. Buy plastic organizers meant for silverware storage. Choose styles with vertical segments—not spoon-shaped slots—to hold large spools of thread on their sides or small spools standing up. Use these organizers to hold marking tools, rulers, seam rippers, scissors and rotary cutters.

If space is at a premium in your studio, place board shelves supported by adjustable brackets on a spare wall. Use clear plastic boxes to store fabric remnants, trims and sewing tools, and stack them on the shelves. Think of these as see-through removable drawers on shelves. Here's how I use mine.

One plastic "drawer" contains only white and off-white remnants, neatly pressed. The next holds pastels. Other "drawers" separate small, medium and large prints. Lower drawers contain solid and darker fabrics. I can see the contents at all times, yet the drawers keep the fabrics organized and clean.

Flat-fold yardage sits on narrow wall shelves spaced a foot apart. Before storing, I wash and press each length. I label each piece with the fabric content. Storing flat-folds on shelves placed close together helps me avoid landslides that occur when the fabric I want is on the bottom of a tall stack. You will find many wonderful ideas for setting up your studio in the series, "Sew Suite," by Jeannie Spears (Sew Suite, *Quilter's Newsletter*, issues #279–#282, 1996).

If you have converted a bedroom to a studio, treasure the closet but not for hanging clothes. You can place additional shelves above the usual existing shelf, giving you storage space all the way to the closet ceiling. Think about purchasing used plywood and compressed fiberboard bookcases and fitting them into the closet. Full of fabric, patterns, books and sewing supplies, their inelegant styling becomes invisible. Nothing beats a walk-in closet with shelves from floor to ceiling.

Storing quilt batting challenges us more than any other item. Consider rolling it into tight tubes. Place these in a clear plastic bag with a label defining the fiber content, overall size and thickness. This eliminates unrolling every batt you own while searching for what you need.

Small desktop cabinets with nesting drawers meant to hold screws and nails are perfect for buttons, snaps, hooks and other tiny items. Most feature plastic drawers, enabling you to see the contents without opening each drawer. Several companies produce organizer boxes with trays of subdivided sections. Look for them in fabric, craft and quilt shops.

ORGANIZING QUILT MAGAZINES

Quilters love quilt magazines, but they can be hard to store. Piling them in stacks on closet shelves or stuffing them into baskets creates havoc when you need a particular issue. Here is an idea for managing your magazine collection. As you read each magazine, make notes on the cover about the articles you found of importance. For example:

p. 21—how to launder quilts

p. 27—request more information about this product

p. 42—find this book in library

p. 61—refer to this ad for color scheme for quilt

p. 75—good article about storing antique quilts

This immediately lets you know why you saved the magazine, ending the need to thumb through many issues looking for something you read months earlier. Consider tossing publications that have no such notations on the covers. This tells you the magazine is not worth saving unless you wish to collect all the issues of a particular subscription.

Store your periodicals by year so you can easily locate a specific issue. Buying slip-cases from publishers is expensive. Consider purchasing inexpensive school-style binders. Another option is a plastic, slotted, three-hole-punched strip. The strips are placed in a binder and the magazines slip into the slots through the center fold, without requiring you to punch holes in the periodical. The strips cost around $3 per set and hold twelve magazines per binder. Label each binder with the magazine title it contains plus the year. Stand the binders neatly on your bookshelf so they are ready for you to find what you need at a moment's notice.

Last, the ultimate secret of organization! *Always* return each item you used from your studio to its proper place so you can find it the next time. An organized studio invites you to do your best work.

Supplies: What Do You Really Need?

Quilting for profit requires you to keep basic supplies available. Hobbyists may have the time to jump in their cars to shop for a single spool of thread, but even as a part-time professional, your time means money. Save time by having these fifteen essentials on hand:

1. Sewing machine, which includes serges or quilting machines if you use them. Keep your machines in good condition by servicing them frequently.
2. Work surface for cutting and laying out projects.
3. Reliable iron, ironing board and other pressing equipment.
4. Template materials.
5. If space allows, a design wall covered with felt or other material enabling you to

temporarily adhere fabric patches and blocks. If you find you cannot spare a wall, here's my solution. Buy a four-foot-square piece of fiberboard, cover it with self-adhering quilt batting and store it beneath a bed or behind a door. Prop it on a chair or against other furniture when needed.

6. Scissors and shears in several sizes plus rotary cutting equipment. Don't get caught with a deadline approaching to find your only rotary blade is dull. Keep spares on hand. Better yet, keep a rotary blade sharpener with your sewing notions like I do.

7. Ordinary sewing notions such as needles, thimbles, regular and silk pins.

8. Marking pens and pencils in several colors for fabric marking that are easily removable.

9. A wide variety of colored quilting, basting and sewing threads.

10. Measuring tapes, rulers, yardsticks and modern quilting cutting guides.

11. Drafting equipment, paper, compass, protractor, French curves, colored pencils, freezer and graph paper for designing.

12. Stencils and stencil-making materials.

13. Batting in several thicknesses and fiber contents.

14. Well-organized, washed and pressed fabric collection.

15. Well-organized patterns, magazine collection and quilting books.

For more ideas on creating the perfect sewing/quilting area, consider the book, *Sewing Room Design*, listed in chapter ten of this book.

Office Equipment: What's Important?

Your business address starts at your desk—literally. Choose a comfortable desk with sufficient surface area for writing and correspondence. Ideally, retain the desktop for active work. Do not allow stacks of paper and correspondence to collect here.

Organize the drawers for office essentials such as stationery, forms, stamps, pens, pencils and so on. Again, consider plastic utensil trays for your desk drawers to eliminate continual searching for items you cannot find. Stackable-trays on a corner of your desk make it easy to separate correspondence, bills, announcements, invoices and other important business papers. Experts suggest that you place your phone on the side of your desk opposite your dominant hand. Thus, if you're right-handed, place the phone on your left so you are prepared to answer with your left hand and make notes with your right.

Modern technology has provided home-based workers with equipment that our forefathers would have envied. Today, many home workers list the items below as indispensable.

• Computers in the home office have become a fixture for many home-based workers. Quilters find them invaluable not just for book work, but for writing instructions and patterns. Modern quilting software enables you to design, color, enlarge, reduce and literally create an entire quilt by computer before beginning the work itself. (See "Resources" at the end of this book for itemized listings of available software.)

• Fax machines provide us with a wonderful way to communicate quickly. Stand-alone styles wired to a dedicated phone line surpass those built into your computer as they remain "on call" twenty-four hours per day.

• IRS regulations state that you may not deduct anything other than toll calls if you have only one telephone in your home. To deduct a business phone plus answering machine and other services such as call-waiting, you *must* have a second phone with a new number brought into your home. Extension phones to your personal phone line do not qualify. Additionally, most phone companies will contact you when they find you are conducting business from a residential phone line.

Here is what you can't live without in your office:
• A desk wide enough to provide a work area and office storage
• A comfortable chair to properly support your back during long sitting periods
• A filing system, which can range from an office filing cabinet to cardboard file boxes that will hold manila folders
• A telephone
• A typewriter, word processor or computer. Many vendors and others with whom you deal do not take handwritten business correspondence on personal stationery seriously
• Bookcases or shelving to store literature, patterns and magazines
• General office supplies such as paper, envelopes, pens, pencils and so on

These are the essentials. As your business grows and your budget permits, you can add to this list. And as your business grows, you may outgrow a combined working studio and business office. If you have the space, two distinct rooms are ideal. Having faced the dilemma myself, I now use a spare bedroom for my studio and a converted double garage as an office. Each area qualifies for the home office deduction following IRS statutes. But whatever available space you have, once everything you need is in one, quiet place, you're on the road to *Make Your Quilting Pay for Itself.*

CHAPTER 1 CHECKLIST

✓ Consider the Small Business Administration's (SBA) personality traits for successful entrepreneurs. Self-motivation, reliability and the ability to work on your own head the list. You must also be prompt, conscientious and well organized. Does this describe you?

✓ Preparation is vital. Have you planned a flexible but efficient work schedule? How are your time management skills? Brush them up if you want to succeed.

✓ Part of good organization requires you to have a comfortable, well-equipped place in which to work. How does your office measure up?

- Do you have all the equipment you need to insure productivity?
- How about your sewing studio? Do you have a place for everything?
- Do you keep your studio well-stocked so you have everything on hand that you need?

✓ Defining your goals is the first step in achieving them. Take time to outline your goals, comparing them frequently with your day-to-day activities. Try to spend most of your time working on tasks that lead directly to your goals.

✓ Consider getting a separate phone line for your business. Phone companies in most cities will insist upon it when they learn you are conducting a business from a personal phone line.

✓ Treat your quilting activities like a business as you make the transition from hobby to profitable enterprise. You will read later that the IRS expects you to make every effort to earn a profit if you want to deduct expenses.

JULIE HIGGINS—
MODERN-DAY
MAIL-ORDER
ENTREPRENEUR

Julie Higgins serves as an excellent example of what preparation and attention to detail can do. Her organization and careful selection and stocking of quilt fabric established her as a successful entrepreneur using all of today's modern technology.

Entering the quilt world in 1990, Julie Higgins recalls her first reaction. "It became apparent to me that this quilting 'thing' was ready to explode! Even as a new quilter, I contributed to the market growth with my preliminary purchases of fabric, tools and other quilt-related goodies."

Julie felt it was important to greet her children when they came home from school. Starting her own home-based business seemed the perfect answer. Julie admits she had worked at various jobs but none held her interest for very long.

"Craft shows appealed to me, so I spent many hours making things to sell. I focused on ideas for good displays and worked hard. After about a year of this, I acquired a shoulder problem that prevented me from active crafting, but I wanted to remain in a craft-related business."

Julie goes on to describe how she founded her successful, mail-order quilt supplies business. "I had just begun to communicate with a group of quilters on Prodigy. We spent a considerable amount of time moaning about the poor quality and fabric selection available from local stores. Dissatisfaction with available fabric got me thinking," says

Julie. "I felt there must be others who felt like we did."

Research came next. Julie learned that because she had previously established herself as a legitimate craft business, she could buy quilting supplies wholesale. In her quest for supply sources, Julie established a friendship with a saleswoman who sold older—and always popular and in demand—Hoffman brand fabrics marked below wholesale cost to make room for new lines. Pondering how to make the best use of these bargain fabrics, Julie decided to see if she could create a market by developing a clientele of quilters interested in buying older fabrics and then passing the lower prices along to them.

Julie prepared to test the idea of providing discounted fabrics to quilters. She began by inviting twenty-three members of the quilting group she had met online to her home for tea. Toward the end of the afternoon, Julie had dazzled her guests by showing them more than fifty yards of the popular Hoffman fabrics she had acquired. She surprised herself by selling almost every yard. Encouraged by her success, Julie searched out other suppliers, who agreed to sell her bundles of various older fabric lines

at reduced prices. So began Julie's mail-order business.

Showing an entrepreneur's pluck, Julie approached her bank. She secured a $5,000 loan co-signed by her husband with his truck as collateral.

Many online quilters posted details recounting their frustrations about trying to buy fabric and quilt-related items while living in rural towns. To get started, Julie decided to focus on serving them to test her market. She had corresponded with many of them for months and they thought of her as a friend. From their comments, she learned what supplies quilters in isolated areas wanted. This helped her establish her niche in the marketplace early. "From the very beginning, I focused on customer service," declares Julie. "If a customer needed something and I didn't have it, I promised to get it!"

Overt advertising is not permitted in online chat groups, but Julie's reputation continued to flourish anyway. Satisfied customers could and did openly discuss and recommend the products she provided and stressed her excellent service. Julie's only advertising was to pass out flyers at quilt shows letting people know about her online services. Having established a presence on the In-

ternet, she became known for being able to find whatever people needed. Online quilters referred their noncomputing friends to her as well. As Julie says, "Never underestimate the importance of word-of-mouth advertising."

Next, Julie identified a new target market. An online quilter stationed with the armed forces in Japan contacted her and asked if Julie could supply her fellow guild members with quilting products. These quilters too, encountered problems trying to purchase materials from a distance. Recognizing that quilters serving in the armed forces abroad were an untapped market, Julie focused on meeting their needs. "Again, my only advertising was word of mouth," says Julie. "I found quilting guilds all over the world located on army and navy bases as one satisfied group would refer me to another.

"I established a contact person with each guild to whom I sent binders listing the fabrics, books and notions I could provide. In turn, she shared the information with members of her guild abroad. She took their orders and sent them to me. We all agreed that everyone benefitted.

"I filled the orders and sent them back to the contact person to distribute to buyers of her guild.

Thus, these quilters gained access to products not available in the countries where they were stationed." Today, Julie continues to serve quilters in the armed services through her online contacts and her World Wide Web site.

"My early success prompted me to begin going to quilt shows. In the midst of trying to build a business on a shoestring, I had become quite addicted to quilting. I found shows everywhere and didn't want to miss any of them. I began to travel to other parts of the country to see what people there were doing."

Traveling to shows inspired Julie with another idea to grow her business. As a vendor at these shows, she could write off travel expenses while visiting states where she had never been before.

Julie ventured further and further from home, a little at a time. She attended regional then national shows. Personally meeting people with whom she'd already been doing business provided Julie with great satisfaction. She loved putting faces to longtime customers she'd served online. People attending the shows and seeing her products also became new mail-order customers, adding to her successful enterprise.

In February 1995, one of Julie's overseas military customers invited her to join a team of designers who were submitting a proposal to the Microsoft Corporation, which wanted to add a craft/hobby arena to their network. Happily, the team's proposal was accepted. Julie joined with other online quilters to sell quilting products on Microsoft's new online service, MSN, which provided a craft mall and bulletin board. Her experiences and contacts there eventually led her to establish her own online enterprise, QC Books. "I specialize in selling crafting and quilting books, enabling me to sell worldwide!" Julie exclaims with pride.

"I am not getting rich from this business and sometimes work more than part time. But I have been to places I had never visited before, and my business pays my expenses to get there. I have satisfied my personal quilting addiction with the latest books, tools and fabrics, and my business pays for them as well. My business provides mini-vacations for my husband and me as I travel to quilt shows. He helps at the shows and when they are over, we often stay a couple of extra days to relax and see the sights in a new area.

"For example, last year we decided to drive to Houston for Quilt Market. Along the way, we stopped and explored caverns, small towns, the mountains and sites we probably never would seen otherwise. My quilting business made it all possible."

Julie Higgins: Quilters Corner

P.O. Box 2024, Martinez, CA 94553

Phone/fax:

(510) 228-2940

E-mail:

QC_Inc@msn.com

Website:

http://www.qcx.com

CHAPTER TWO

GETTING STARTED

Beginning a new business, especially in a field you have enjoyed as a hobby, requires careful planning. Take a look at the time you have available to start your new business. Does your daily schedule provide enough time to quilt for profit or must you rearrange your weekly and monthly calendar? Once you've decided that you want to use your quilting skills to make money, you must determine how many weekly hours you can devote to your new enterprise. Will you work part time or full time, from home or from a shop? Let's examine these alternatives.

Working Part Time

Beginning part time and building your business slowly provides you with several important advantages. You will find it easier to:

- Become established
- Gather business experience
- Determine whether quilting as an income-producing activity is right for you
- Test the market to learn if a demand exists for what you plan to offer

Working Full Time

If you decide to begin your business on a full-time basis, you must:

- Make sure you can work a full day without interruptions
- Arrange for child care if you still have small children at home
- Have a well-organized work schedule in place

Working From Home

Working from home isn't a fad—it is here to stay. Books, newsletters and catalogs dedicate themselves to the home-based worker and recognize this as a large and lucrative market. They continually address the most common problem you will face when you work where you live: learning to separate your personal time from your business tasks.

If you begin your quilting business from home, you may hear this: "How nice that you can stay at home and work, but is quilting really *work*? Isn't it more like getting paid to play? It must be so easy." Working from home can become complicated. Here's why:

- Society programs us to associate home with family, rest, relaxation and everyone's favorite—housework.
- Conversely, society expects that working from a job site means leaving home interests behind each day, clearly separating these interests from income-producing work.

Commuting from breakfast in your kitchen to your studio does not provide much time to switch identities from resident to worker. The short trip blurs which identity you have at a given moment. Several generations have socialized us to keep this clean-cut separation, but it has not always been so. Before the industrial revolution, working from home was the norm. Today, as we return to this lifestyle of working out of the house, our generation must learn how to do it without the benefit of role models from generations past.

When you work where you live, one of two extremes may prevail. You may either relax too much, giving most of your attention to home/family issues, or you may become a workaholic.

When you begin working from home, it is easy to squander your time on unaccustomed, unrestricted domestic relaxation. When the day runs short, you may find yourself rushing to squeeze in professional duties.

On the other hand, you may find it hard to stop working at what you love since your work is so accessible. To maintain a happy home, guard against spending all of your energy on professional duties at the expense of your family.

The secret of success is to focus on who we are at a given moment and to do the appropriate task at hand. Mix in a large dose of time management and self-discipline to keep personal tasks separate from professional duties and your new quilting business will thrive.

Assess Your Current Workload

Take time to examine your present schedule. Only then can you determine how much time you can set aside for your new profit-making venture. Let's look at some possible scenarios that might describe your situation:

• *You have a full-time job outside of your home.* You plan to work on your quilting business three evenings per week and most of each weekend.

• *You have a part-time job outside of your home.* Perhaps you can set aside two whole days for your new business plus several weekday evenings.

• *You have a part-time, home-based job.* How demanding is it? Can you shuffle your time by setting aside a specific period—mornings, for example—for your present job and afternoons for your new quilting endeavors? Or maybe reversing this will work for you.

• *You are retired, a stay-at-home mom or presently not working for pay.* If this describes you, don't automatically assume you don't need to plan. To the contrary, if you have unlimited time, you must carefully plan and organize your time, for now it will count even more. If you have not had to organize your time for a while, you may find it takes time to train yourself to maintain a work schedule.

• *You have minor to major health constraints and feel working outside your home is no longer possible.* Setting up your own work schedule to accommodate your needs and limitations can be the perfect solution if you desire a part-time income while reserving time for the rest you need. If this is the case, perhaps you can work the first four hours of the day, then lie down to read, study or rest and then return to quilting tasks for another hour or two later.

Learn to Use Your Time More Efficiently

Since no one has more than twenty-four hours per day, absorbing your new business activities into your present schedule may challenge your organizational skills. Find new time for your business by eliminating time-wasters and combining mundane tasks. Here are a few time-savers that may help:

• Combine TV watching with the mundane tasks of your business such as basting, pressing, hand-stitching or other less demanding activities.

• Leave mindless chores by the phone to be done only when *you* choose to talk on the phone. For example, leave a basket of laundry to fold; projects requiring hand-basting or ripping; or letters to stuff, fold and seal. Such tasks do not require your full attention, but after a few calls, they will appear to have been done as if by magic at the end of the day.

• Speaking of the phone, consider purchasing a one-hundred-foot cord or a cellular phone, enabling you to walk around while you talk. Water your plants, dust or iron if you choose to talk. I often prepare food when on the phone and have been known to clean my refrigerator shelves, one at a time, when engaged in lengthy conversations.

You must learn to balance how much money you need or want to earn with the time you have available to incorporate income-generating activities into your week. Be realistic. You probably cannot earn $300 working only ten to fifteen hours per week. However, you may earn that amount in a month if you devote a regular amount of time to your income-producing quilting.

What's Your Specialty?

We could all spend a lifetime trying to learn every possible quilting technique and still not manage to do so. To begin earning money in the quilting field, begin with what you already know. What are your areas of expertise? Here's a list to get you thinking. I'm sure you can add to it.

- Quiltmaking
- Full-sized bed quilts
- Wall hangings
- Pillows
- Accessories
- Wearable patchwork
- Stuffed toys and animals
- Traditional pieced quilts
- Appliqué
- Art quilts
- Scrap quilts
- Contemporary quilts
- Pattern making
- Fabric printing, dyeing, marbling
- Teaching
- Quilt restoration
- Can work in many styles
- Services for others (see chapter eight for more ideas)
- Designing for magazine publication (see chapter six for details)

Turning Your Specialty Into a Niche in the Marketplace

Choosing which aspects of quilting appeal to you will help you determine your specialty. Once you've singled out one or more specialties, do your homework. Study and practice until you reach a level of proficiency and expertise.

Your next step is to assess how your specialty fits into the existing marketplace. Since you cannot serve the entire quilting industry, identify what part of the market will benefit you the most. Accomplish this by doing your own market research.

Begin by studying and comparing the major quilting magazines available today. Analyze current trends, and read letters and questions sent to the editor by readers who want to learn more. Study the classified ads to learn what people are buying and what others offer for sale. Request copies of quilt catalogs to see what they offer. Catalogs are expensive, so most are market-driven. This means the pages contain only what consumers want to buy as opposed to what the seller wants to sell. (See chapter ten for a list of magazines and catalogs.)

Attend as many local, regional and national quilting events as possible. Note which classes fill to overflowing and which attract only small numbers of students. Learn what topics popular teachers offer and which seminars and lectures keep the audience's attention. This will help you know "what's hot and what's not." After completing your market research, you will be in a better position to create a market-driven product or service yourself—one that will satisfy a recognized need.

To learn how you can stand out from the crowd, answer these questions:

- What's special about your work?
- What can you do that no one else or very few others are doing?
- Have you heard about successful quilting-related services in other parts of the country that don't exist in your community?
- Do they appeal to you?

Read the nine profiles at the end of each chapter in this book and note how each person created a special niche in the marketplace following her market research. At the end of this chapter, you will meet Millie Becker, a quilter who targets a very specific market. She knows that no one can reach every American consumer, but she has found excellent ways to reach likely buyers of her products—those confined to wheelchairs. In chapter one, you met Julie Higgins. Remember her creativity in locating a special niche in a worldwide market—quilters stationed overseas? What position can you develop for yourself?

Once you have defined your niche in the marketplace, you will be better able to:
- Locate the most likely customers for your product or service
- Advertise and promote your business where it will do the most good
- Know what to read and where to find help and information
- Focus your effort and energy in the direction most likely to be profitable
- Avoid becoming too scattered and diversified, which may minimize success

Chapter three will help you learn about marketing techniques and how to identify and reach your target consumers.

Making a Profit

Everyone wants a foolproof, easy system that guarantees maximum profit with minimum waste of resources. Unfortunately, no such formula exists, but you can create and implement a variety of fee-setting methods to suit your individual situation and geographical area. You must devise a fee schedule that brings in reasonable profit for your efforts and one you can live with as your business grows.

Minimize Your Expenses

Purchasing supplies for your office and quilting/sewing materials for your studio will become major expenses. Minimizing such expenses while maintaining a well-stocked office and studio may be a challenge. Here are two ideas that may help:
- Pay wholesale prices for everything you buy for resale. Buying supplies "on sale" at a retail store may be appropriate for hobbyists, but you will profit more by earning the difference between wholesale costs and the retail price your consumer pays you.
- Before you buy office equipment and supplies, shop around for the lowest possible prices by checking discount stores, chain office supply stores and mail-order houses.

Setting Your Fees

Begin your fee-setting efforts by checking with competitors in your community. Learn what other teachers, designers and quilters charge for their services. Examine their classified ads in local newspapers. Visit quilt shops and learn what they charge for services and products comparable to yours. Consult the phone directory to call other quilt professionals and request price quotes.

Later in this chapter, I will offer several price-setting options, but before providing them, let's make sure you understand the four principal elements to consider as you set prices: labor, raw materials, overhead and profit.

1. *Labor* is the time you spend producing your product or service. Determine what your time is worth by answering these questions: How much do you need to make? How many hours must you devote to your work to earn this amount? Are your skills at a professional level?

Many people beginning a business tend to underestimate the value of their time. Think carefully as you define how much time it takes to produce a product or service. Do not diminish the value of your labor by setting a price that is too low. If you are willing to settle for $4 per hour because you're at home with your children, what will happen when you receive an unexpectedly large order, making it necessary to hire someone to help you? Will another worker accept $4 per hour? When you consider labor, think about what you would realistically have to pay someone else to help you when needed.

2. *Raw materials* are the supplies required to manufacture your product. Fabric and batting come to mind, but don't forget to consider small items such as glue, needles, thread and pins.

3. *Overhead* is the nonproductive, incidental expenses too small to calculate individually such as utilities, postage, wear and tear on your sewing machine, travel, repairs and maintenance.

4. *Profit* refers to the amount of money you wish to earn per unit after you deduct the three pricing elements above.

Pricing Example

Let's say that you have been commissioned to design and make a quilted wall hanging. How would you calculate the fee? In our example, the customer wants a wall hanging that measures three feet square. The client is not knowledgeable about the time or skill required, but has specifically asked for a floral design in appliqué with an all-over grid pattern, hand-quilted for the background.

| Raw materials: | Two yards of fabric for a quilt top in several colors | $ 14.00 |
| | 1½ yards of fabric for backing @ $6 per yard | $ 9.00 |

One bag of batting, crib-size	$ 2.49
One spool of quilting thread	$ 2.00
Three spools of sewing threads	$ 4.00
New pencil to mark design	$ 1.29
Stencil chosen by customer	$ 2.99
	_____
	$ 35.77

Now let's say you want to charge $8 per hour. To make the quilt top, you have calculated that it will take you approximately eighteen hours to make an easy design with a few, large shapes; twenty-two hours to make one a little more complex; and twenty-five hours for a more intricate shape. Rounding off fractions, your fee schedule could look like this.

	Simple design	Medium design	Intricate design
Labor:	$150	$175	$200
Hand-quilting:	Lines at least 1″ apart	Lines at least ½″ apart	Stippling
	$ 50	$ 85	$125
Drafting original design:	$ 25	$ 40	$ 60

If you sum up the appropriate totals based on the medium design, the final price to make the quilt would be $300 plus materials and factoring in overhead expenses and the time needed to draft the design.

Study the price schedule above and compare it with what the market will bear in your area. If you live in New York, where handwork is prized and highly valued, you may have no trouble charging this amount. But suppose you live in a small farming community where many people quilt and there are frequent shows with quilts for sale. You may need to drop your price to compete with the current local market.

A Word About Overhead

Large companies have bookkeepers to painstakingly calculate actual overhead expenses item by item. Home-based people usually find itemizing overhead expenses a complicated process since overhead constitutes such a small portion of their total expenses. Here's a shortcut suggested by the book, *Women Working Home*.

Divide the total amount of raw materials consumed for a single unit of the product or service into thirds. Estimate your overhead expense as one-third of the raw materials total amount. For example, raw materials for a quilted pillow include fabric, lining, thread and stuffing for a total of $9. Take one-third of this amount—$3—for overhead, which might include such expenses as wear and tear on your sewing machine and iron plus the electricity you used, a portion of your insurance expenses, travel to a quilt shop for materials, and so on.

Thus, the fee would look like this:

Labor:	Three hours @ $8 per hour	$ 24
Raw materials:		$ 9
Overhead:	one-third of raw materials	$ 3
		——
Totals:		$ 36

Before estimating your overhead expenses using this system, check with your tax preparer. He or she should be your final guide on whether calculating overhead expenses this way fits in with the other business costs reported on your annual federal income tax return.

Let's see how this system works when using Barbara Brabec's system described below.

Barbara Brabec's Pricing Formula

In her book, *Creative Cash,* Barbara Brabec presents a shortcut pricing formula used by many craftspeople. She suggests totaling your figures for labor, raw materials and overhead to determine a wholesale price and then doubling this amount to arrive at the full retail price.

Referring back to the quilted pillow, which totaled $36 for labor, raw materials and overhead, Barbara's method would mean that $36 would be the wholesale amount. Doubling this amount to $72 provides the retail price. Bear in mind that when you sell at wholesale, you should set a minimum order amount for vendors who buy pillows from you. Though you make less than you would selling the individual pillows at full retail, you make up the difference in volume sales by allowing assembly line sewing methods to be used to produce the pillows, thus cutting the labor time.

Using a Pricing Range

Making quilts for sale is the sole occupation of a quilter I spoke to recently. Though she uses a different system to arrive at her prices, they are surprisingly similar to ones arrived at by using the method above. Note that in making a similar wall quilt, she, too, would charge from $100 to $175 depending on the degree of difficulty. Each price bracket includes a range based on whether the piecing is simple to intricate. Here is her system. For labor only, she charges for:

Miniatures:	$125-$150
Wall quilts:	$100-$175
Full-sized bed quilts:	$350-$500

Pricing by the Square Foot

Another quilter who lives near me in California uses an interesting formula to set prices. She determines the square foot measurement and multiplies it by $20 for easy design/work, $25 for medium design work and $30 for complex designs. I used her method to price a quilt I made recently. Here is how the method worked out.

My quilt measured $36'' \times 42''$ or 1,512 square inches. I divided this by 144 inches—the equivalent of one square foot—and came up with 10.5 feet Since my quilt featured intricate appliqué and hand-quilting, I multiplied $30 by 10.5 feet and charged $315 to do the work, plus raw materials.

Out of curiosity, I researched past records and found I had made a quilt with approximately the same measurements two years ago. The design featured fabric painting, piecing and quilting, all by hand. The publisher of a nationally known craft magazine had paid me $300 for my work. Since publishers customarily return quilts and other projects after photography, I had the option of keeping or reselling it. Though I had not heard before of the system described above, it proved to me that the publisher had paid me a fair price.

Charging by the Spool of Quilting Thread

Nonprofit quilt guilds, church groups and others set their prices by charging by the spool of quilting thread. (Currently this price is $100 in California, but call within your state to determine current prices.) When a client wants a quilt top hand-quilted, the price depends on the amount of thread consumed. Large quilts with minimal hand-quilting may cost the same as small wall hangings bearing profuse, close quilting lines. The concept is simple: It takes the same amount of thread to make a given amount of stitches, be they widely spaced or close together.

Charging by the Hour

Consider charging by the hour. Set your minimum hourly fee and multiply by the units needed. For example, if it takes you three hours to cut, piece, stitch and baste one 14″ block and you charge $6 per hour, you would charge $18 per block. If your customer ordered the same block on a king-sized quilt composed of twenty-four blocks, you would charge $432 for everything except the quilting ($18 × 24 = $432 for seventy-two hours of work). To do the quilting, you can negotiate whether the buyer wants it done by hand or by machine and charge accordingly.

Charging by Yardage

Another idea is to charge by the yardage consumed in your labor. For example, if a quilt consumes eight total yards of fabric for the top alone and you base your fee on $7 per yard, you would charge a total of $56. If you set your labor at $8 per yard, you would charge a total of $448 to make the quilt.

Choosing Your Own Pricing Method

A well-known quilter I know sticks by a basic hourly formula that works well for her: She charges $50 per square foot plus materials. To find a price-setting formula perfect for you, try this. Choose a quilt project you might undertake in your business. Price fabrics and other needed materials in your area. Set up a mock materials cost list like the one shown earlier.

Now, price this quilt project using each system described above. Take the resulting price from each system and add them together. Divide by the number of systems you used and you will have an average of all the systems. Then visit quilting events and shops in your community. How does the resulting price fit in your geographical area? Is it higher or lower than the market will bear? Is it competitive with other quilters nearby? Perhaps it will provide you with a practical fee schedule you can live with for quite some time.

Regardless of the formula you choose, you must remain sensitive to what your local market will bear. Adjust the final price to accommodate your market.

CHAPTER 2 CHECKLIST

✓ Decide how many hours per week you want to devote to profitable quilting activities.

✓ Select your market. It should be something that you do best and is perhaps an area underserved by other quilt professionals in your community.

✓ Pricing techniques challenge everyone. Which system presented appeals to you? Perhaps you can combine some of the ideas as you create your own system. Take care not to undervalue your time as you begin your business.

MILLIE BECKER—A
VERY SPECIAL NICHE
IN THE MARKETPLACE

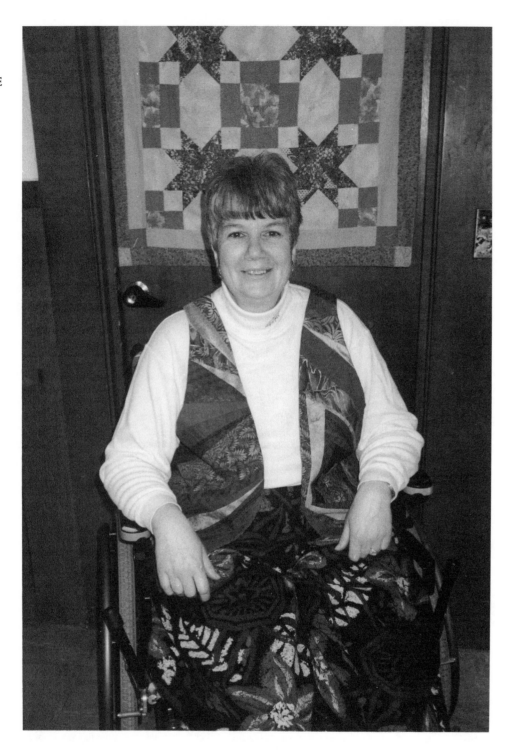

Millie Becker always enjoyed knitting, crocheting and sewing, but quilting did not attract this Danvers, Massachusetts, resident. Muscular dystrophy changed Millie's life when she was only forty-three years old, not yet finished raising her three children. By 1988, she found she needed to use a wheelchair full time. No longer able to tolerate the small, repetitive motion of knitting or crocheting, Millie took an embroidery class. Her love of handcrafts still appealed to her, and she hoped to find a skill within her physical limitations. Embroidery also proved too painful for her but a woman in the class suggested she consider quilting. "All I knew about quilting at that time was that people cut up old clothes and made them into quilt blankets," admits Millie.

Millie explains that she could not sit idle watching television, so to minimize depression, she followed her friend's suggestion and borrowed a few quilting books from her local library. Quilting renewed her enthusiasm for beautiful handwork, so it did not take long for Millie to exhaust reading all of the quilting books in her local library.

At about this time, Millie increased her mobility by making use of Paratransit transportation (door-to-door van service for those with disabilities) to Boston, twenty miles from home. "The Boston Library had several hundred quilting books," says Millie, "and I wanted to read them all."

Millie spent the next three months reading. Then, in 1991, she decided on her first project: a queen-sized bed quilt! After signing up for her first quilting class, necessity inspired Millie to design her first quilted tote bag for herself.

"Since I did not yet have a power chair, I needed my arms to push my chair," explains Millie. "I made my first bag big enough to carry everything I needed to my quilting class. Wheelchairs seem to have the same type of depressing black or vinyl accessories that just won't lay flat. I designed mine to remain snug against the back of the chair no matter how much I stuffed into it."

Her first sale came from a friend who asked Millie to make a quilt for her new grandchild. She worked diligently on a panda quilt from the book, *Patchwork Quilts to Make for Children*, by Margaret Rolfe. After completing it, her therapist from her support group saw it and commissioned her to make a queen-sized, pieced flower quilt.

"I was so excited that someone would pay me $450 to make a quilt that didn't even have to be laboriously hand-quilted—just tied. Jerry, my husband, helped with the sashing borders as they challenged my arm strength. All the while, I sported my bag on the back of my wheelchair everywhere I went."

It didn't take long for other wheelchair users to ask Millie to make her beautiful tote bags for them. Millie became even more determined to take the "drab" out of wheelchair accessories. She wanted wheelchair-bound customers to enjoy bold, bright, beautiful colors with intricate designs. As a wheel-

chair user herself, she understood the needs of others who required mobility devices.

Millie's bags are machine-pieced and fully lined with an inside pocket—perfectly suited to her special market. She uses only 100 percent prewashed cotton fabrics to avoid shrinkage.

Today, Millie works part time making beautiful wheelchair bags and other accessories for the disabled. Since her niche in the marketplace is tightly focused, Millie attends trade shows as many of us do, but hers are very specialized. For example, she has rented booth space for the last three years at the Assistive Technology Show in the World Trade Center in Boston.

Millie searched for ideas to make her work easier. QuiltPro software helps Millie design quilts. Cutting and making quilt templates with scissors can be a challenge to a person with limited muscle control. Rotary cutters are the perfect answer for Millie. Paper-piecing techniques eliminate many steps in the quilt-making process for her as well. "Combining these methods, I can do a bag in a week much easier and faster," exclaims Millie enthusiastically.

Quilting may be the central focus of her life, but Millie finds quilting has also led her to developing computer skills. Since getting her first computer two years ago, her quilting life has broadened. "Online quilters enable me to make friendships, since quilt guilds in my area are too far away for me to travel to and most of them are not wheelchair accessible," explains Millie.

Millie credits her online capability with providing her with a virtual community of quilters all over the U.S. "Communicating with other online quilters means so much to me," says Millie. She participates in fabric swaps and exchanges tips and information about quilt products and books. "Before I went online, I was a sole, lonely quilter due to inaccessibility. Now online quilters have become my quilt guild and they have taught me so much—they've changed my life."

Millie eagerly shares her latest news, which is success by anyone's standards. Her first original art quilt designed by computer and made using paper-piecing methods was accepted as part of a quilt exhibit. Though Millie may not travel around the U.S., her quilt certainly is doing so as the exhibit moves across the country.

Due to her limited physical energy, Millie does not envision herself as a full-time quilt designer. However, if demand warrants it, she has a contingency plan. She will hire other disabled people to help. Millie Becker serves as an inspiration to all that persistence, determination, ingenuity and good marketing can equal a successful, most "able" quilting entrepreneur.

SPECIAL NOTE

While revising this book for publication in October 1996, I received the following update from Millie Becker. I felt compelled to share it with my readers.

On October 23, 1996, Millie received a letter from the American Quilting Society that far exceeded her quilting expectations to date. The editor of the AQS magazine plans to feature Millie's first originally designed quilt in an upcoming issue. Millie, still flying high, wrote to me describing her reaction.

"This is my first totally original design and my first machine-quilted piece. I thoroughly enjoyed the designing process, including the complex angles I designed on QuiltPro. I designed it as a single block, printing out each patch to use as a pattern for paper-piecing construction. I didn't enjoy the quilting as much as the designing and piecing, as it was difficult for me to handle it due to my limited mobility. Without QuiltPro, I never could have designed it, let alone sewn it. Without Maurine Noble's book, *Machine Quilting Made Easy*, I could not have handled the bulk of the completed quilt with my diminished arm strength." Is it possible for any of us to fail to be moved and inspired after reading Millie's words?

MILLIE BECKER: QUILTED CREATIONS

31 Clark Street, Danvers, MA 01923

Phone:

(508) 777-2613

E-mail:

enrgi8a@prodigy.com

FINDING CUSTOMERS

Marketing does *not* mean selling. Marketing precedes both advertising and selling. Successful selling can only take place *after* researching the current market which, in turn, helps you identify and find your most likely customers. Just what does the word "marketing" mean? Marketing is a never-ending business process of evaluating what works and what doesn't, what's wanted and what's not. I call this "becoming aware of the external marketplace"—developing a sensitivity toward producing what customers want to buy rather than what you want to sell. Avoid the common notion many new business owners often have about marketing—that customers are as enthused about buying your product as you are selling it to them.

Marketing reality begins by realizing that no single product appeals to everyone. To find your ideal customers, you must assess the size of the total potential market followed by identifying where your quilting product or service fits in. Incidentally, if your business offers a service rather than a product for sale, don't assume marketing does not apply to you. Service *is* your product!

Not every potential buyer of quilt products and services will buy from you. Therefore, you must ask yourself, "What segment of the market will buy?" Defining your target market means identifying the group of available buyers most likely to show an interest in what you have to offer.

Why You Need a Marketing Plan

Full- or part-time business owners who want to succeed know the wisdom of drafting a marketing plan to outline and organize marketing and advertising strategies. Saying that your marketing plan "is in your head" reveals that you have not taken its value seriously. Without a plan, you will have little direction, no stated goals and no way to measure and recognize your success.

Your Marketing Plan Should

- Be in writing
- Be updated annually
- Always consider the changeability of the external marketplace
- Have defined objectives
- Include an implementation timetable
- Be clear, precise and easy to understand
- Be practical and realistic
- Be flexible and adaptable to change
- Be as complete as you can make it

Creating Your Plan

To start creating your plan, sit down with a pencil and paper and write out the answers to these questions:

1. What business are you in? What do you want to sell? Be specific. For example, don't just say "quilts." Answer whether you plan to design, make, teach, restore or sell quilts.
2. Does a demand exist for your product or service? How do you know? (*Hint:* Read the major craft, quilting and trade journals.)
3. Why will your product or service sell? Can you describe at least three of its principal benefits for the consumer?
4. Describe your potential customers: Who are they? Where do they live?
5. What advertising and promotions methods will reach them? What do they read? (*Hint:* Find out by requesting writers' guidelines from prominent craft, quilting and sewing magazines. These guidelines will describe the magazines' readerships and offer demographic data.)
6. Find out about your competition. Where are they?
7. What makes your product/service better than theirs?
8. Read your competition's advertisements. Can you determine the benefit of their products or services for the customer?
9. How do your prices compare with the competition?
10. What products do they carry? What services do they offer?
11. Who are their vendors, distributors, wholesalers or retailers? Visiting their location and scrutinizing their sales literature and catalogs will help you determine the answers to the last three questions.

Before probing into the questions listed above, consider one more point. Will your product or service be market- or product-driven? Market-driven products are aimed at satisfying an established and desired need in the market. A current example in the quilting world centers around quilt batts. Customers (the market) have increased their demand for batts made of natural fibers such as cotton and wool. Producing these in greater quantities, sizes and styles would fit the definition of market-driven.

Product-driven items usually do not fare as well in the marketplace. Product-driven companies often insist upon selling what they *want* to produce as opposed to producing what the market wants. Using our quilt batt example again, a product-driven company may decide that polyester is cheaper to manufacture and weighs less than natural fibers. To ignore the growing market demand for natural fibers would undoubtedly lead to lower sales of polyester batts as people are presently turning away from them in favor of natural fibers.

Market- or Product-Driven

Let's say you plan to design and make quilts to sell. If your line is product-driven, you would stress product benefits in your advertising. For example, you might underscore that you use the most economical batts available. You might also assure customers that you guarantee that your quilts are colorfast and shrink-resistant. Perhaps you could point out that you will make quilts to fit any bed size and that your wall quilts can be custom ordered to any measurement. Note that all of the above stress the benefits of the product. If this is what customers are buying, you may do well.

However, if you decide on a market-driven quilt business, you would stress how your products and services relate to current trends and preferences. For example, referring to the batts on the market, your advertising might mention that you have added a line of cotton batts in various thicknesses and sizes from which your customers can choose.

Renewed interest in Victorian and Baltimore quilts serve as another example. You would perfect your skills in this area if you want to sell more even if you must set personal preferences aside. Ribbon embroidery to embellish these quilts is also enjoying an unprecedented popularity right now. Thus, to remain current, you would consider adding this technique to your products. Color choices you choose would reflect today's current jewel tones as opposed to the earth tones so popular a generation ago. Market-driven quiltmakers must constantly observe trends and remain flexible enough to respond to them to satisfy consumer demand.

The Color Marketing Group, a nonprofit international association of 1,200 design and color professionals dedicated to forecasting and tracking color/design trends in the U.S., meets twice yearly. They analyze current consumer color preferences and also predict color trends two years in advance. Many craft and quilt seminars offer annual lectures and presentations by a Color Marketing Group representative, or you may reach them at 4001 N. Ninth Street, Suite 102, Arlington, VA 22203 (703) 528-7666 for more information.

Identifying Your Likely Customers

Good marketing techniques require that you have an accurate picture of your likely customers. You need to identify, describe, locate and eventually reach them. You cannot aim your advertising dollars at your targeted customer if you do not understand who they are, what they read, what they need and why they need it. Target marketing contributes greatly to the success of any business large or small.

Your Customer Profile

Creating a profile of your most likely customers is a vital step in your marketing efforts. Here are a few guidelines to follow:

1. Determine if gender affects the purchasing of your product. Generally, quilted items, supplies, books and patterns are bought by women but perhaps your item will appeal to men buying gifts for their wives.

2. Baby boomers—those born between 1946 and 1964—have different buying habits than teenagers or seniors. Ask yourself if people of all age groups will be drawn to your product or if it will appeal primarily to a particular group. For example, hand-quilted baby items and toys will interest new parents and grandparents, but fashionable vests will attract more clothes-conscious younger women. If people of a certain age will be those most interested in buying your product, the language of your advertising, color selection and style must suit their tastes to encourage them to buy. For example, to target seniors specifically, your literature might contain conservative language written on traditional-colored papers. However, if your market reaches out to teenagers, you might use more contemporary or "cool" terms and neon and other bright, modern color schemes that appeal to them.

3. Perhaps a certain educational level is required for buyers to appreciate your product. For example, only computer-literate consumers would be interested in your

new quilting software, but educational level is immaterial if you specialize in quilted items for the kitchen.

4. Economic buying power of your likely customers may be a consideration if you offer primarily high-end art quilts for sale. Buyers must have greater discretionary income and an expressed appreciation of art than, say, those who want only washable, practical bed quilts. Though the latter group still must have dollars, these buyers may more likely be families with children and a more limited income.

Where Do Your Customers Shop?

Once you have a profile of the type of person most likely to show an interest in your product, you need to find out how to reach them. You must ask yourself where your customers would most likely shop. Where would they expect to find items like yours? Some places to consider include:

- Quilt shops
- Quilt shows and exhibits
- Art shows
- Street fairs
- Tourist shopping areas
- County and state fairs

Framed quilt designs appear profusely in quilt shops, but full-sized quilts are more readily found at quilt shows and exhibits. Street fairs may be the ideal place to offer quilted wallets and potholders, but art shows would not be the best choice for these.

Perhaps your customers would respond better to reading about your product. You must decide which magazines they would most likely read. Remember Millie Becker from the last chapter? Placing ads in magazines and newsletters for the disabled, while appropriate for her, may not be for you. However, if you plan to finish quilts for others, advertising in the classified sections of quilt magazines may be a better idea. Their readers are primarily quilters, some of whom may prefer to have their quilts finished for them.

If you plan to design and make quilts for consumers, consider leaving flyers and brochures at local sewing centers. Customers who admire such items but cannot or do not have the time to quilt, often seek referrals from shops where fabric is available for sale.

Consider the importance of online contacts, as Julie Higgins did in chapter one. Perhaps your target buyers might be more apt to find you on a World Wide Web site.

You will find many quilt-related malls, websites and online quilting information in the last chapter of this book.

Getting the Word Out

Once you have identified your target market, the next question to answer is, "How will you reach your customer?" Your choices fall into two basic categories: paid advertising and low-cost promotion.

You have many choices when you pay to advertise. You can place ads in:

- Magazines
- Telephone books
- Trade journals
- Direct mail packages
- Local newspapers

Advertising in Magazines

Generally, advertising offers two alternatives: classified ads where you pay by the word, and display ads where you pay by the size of the space where your information appears. Classified ads accept words only while display ads may include words, your logo, line drawings, sketches and photos.

Classified ads will cost less and generate more sales if you learn to write them as professional writers do, called "tight writing." Simply put, this means using the fewest, strongest words that say the most. Practice writing your ad. Include the essentials: what you have to sell, where the customer can reach you, how they can pay you and what they will pay.

Next, write the ad again, eliminating any unnecessary words. Write it a third time. Try to combine words if possible. Why say "black and white" if you can say "b/w," for example? Write it a fourth time and eliminate prepositions and adverbs. Write it a fifth time using strong, imperative language. Some examples: "Buy now!"; "Don't wait!"; "Order today!" Teach yourself this important skill by reading the book, *Write Tight*, by William Brohaugh.

Though you may think consumer magazines such as *Better Homes & Gardens* or *Sunset* offer the ideal places to advertise, think again. Magazines that focus on home issues and activities are too general for one-person quilting businesses. You may also be shocked when you learn they charge thousands of dollars for color display ads.

Narrow your search instead. Look for magazines such as *Crafts* or *Quilting Today*, which have smaller readerships that focus on your market. They charge less than large, glossy publications while addressing likely buyers more closely.

Writer's Market (Writer's Digest Books) is my favorite source for locating specialty magazines. This annual directory for writers lists hundreds of magazines, many of which could be suitable for you as an advertiser. Identify one or two whose readership matches your target market and you've won half the battle of successful marketing.

Mary-Jo McCarthy, an expert in marketing quilts and other crafts throughout the United States, offers this wise advice. "When a quilter decides to start advertising, she needs to plan a minimum of four ads a year in the same publication. She needs to have the funds to invest and not expect her mailbox to be stuffed with orders when the first ad appears. The ad needs to reflect the product and should always be simple and to the point. Include ordering information in the ad. A new business person can consider the first ad successful if it only recoups the ad cost. Usually, it's the publication of the second or third ad that begins to generate profit."

Telephone Book Display Ads

Once you have a business telephone number, your phone company will automatically list your number in both the white and yellow pages in your local phone directory. (See the next chapter for information about business phones.) However, you may wish to consider broadening this coverage by placing a display ad in the yellow section. You must pay an extra monthly charge, so check your phone directory to learn the costs of different-sized display ads. Remember, unlike classified ads, display ads permit you to include your logo, line drawings and sketches in addition to text. Unquestionably, display ads enhance your credibility as a professional but you will have to weigh this against the monthly charge.

Advertising in Trade Journals and Newsletters

Browse through *The Encyclopedia of Associations*, available in your public library, to find lists of groups, clubs and trade associations that publish trade journals or newsletters. Target a specific group devoted to your specialty. Placing ads in these smaller but highly specialized publications costs much less than advertising in consumer magazines and reaches your target consumer more directly.

Selling by Direct Mail

Mary-Jo McCarthy uses direct mail to follow-up when interested customers request information about her products. "Always have a printed brochure or catalog available to mail promptly upon request," advises Mary-Jo. "Charge for a small brochure or catalog to defray costs. This will sift out people who love to get anything free by mail but never intend to buy."

Selling by direct mail requires extensive research, thorough preparation and comprehension of mail-order techniques and regulations. If selling this way appeals to you, see chapter ten for a listing of books on mail-order selling before proceeding.

Newspaper Advertising

Your local newspaper is the ideal place to begin advertising if your quilting business offers service over product. Since coverage is local, you will reach residents in your own community. Teachers and those who offer quilting services to others find newspaper advertising beneficial. Newspapers also offer both classified and display ads, so before proceeding, check to see how your local competition uses this valuable tool. There is more information on learning about your competitors later in this chapter.

Low- or No-Cost Promotion

Unlike advertising, where you pay dearly to get the word out, promotion costs little to nothing while letting your potential customers know what you have to offer. Here are a few suggestions to get you started. Add to this list as your business grows.

1. Join organizations other than ones in your field such as art groups or business and civic groups. Let members in your community know what you do.
2. Give flyers and brochures to your Chamber of Commerce, which is where new residents go to learn about local products and services.
3. Get a business phone and make sure it is listed in the yellow pages.
4. Send newsletters or flyers to nearby guilds and fabric stores.
5. Place posters or flyers in shops or places where people gather. Check first to see if you need permission to do this.
6. Write a press release for your local newspaper. Make it interesting. Newspapers do not find it worthwhile to publish mundane information. Give your release a special twist that attracts attention.

7. Offer to give demonstrations for local civic, craft and other interested groups at every opportunity.
8. Participate in local fairs and exhibits in your community.
9. Join local and regional quilt and craft groups and start networking.

Check Your Competition

Once you decide exactly what you are going to sell and who you will be selling it to, you must learn all you can about your competition including their strengths and weaknesses. Begin your research by scanning classified ads in local newspapers. Have you found anyone doing what you plan to do? Check the yellow pages in your local phone directory. What other quilting products and services are listed?

What can you offer that they do not? Remember how Julie Higgins targeted her likeliest prospects? She reached out to a group of online quilters located overseas on military bases, a group that was overlooked by traditional sellers.

If no one in your community machine quilts for others, for example, you might fill this need. Conversely, if other professional quilters in your area do only machine quilting, perhaps you can consider specializing in heritage hand-quilting.

San Francisco's Bay Area, where I live, is home to a strong quilting community. One designer I know makes only contemporary quilts on commission. A nearby and successful competitor limits herself to making quilts based on old, traditional patterns using depression-era fabric styles being remanufactured today.

The community college where I teach needlework and quilting has another, well-known quilting teacher on the faculty. There is room for both of us, as she teaches contemporary pieced designs with the completed top hand-quilted on a frame. However, I specialize in no-frame, quilt-as-you-go quilts with a strong bent on appliqué. By assessing your strengths and weaknesses and comparing them to your closest competition, you too may find success developing a complementary specialty with your competition rather than vying for the same customers.

Advertising Your Product or Service

Once you have identified your target customer, think about what advertising style will be most suitable for them. Marketing and advertising experts often reduce an advertising style to three basic alternatives. Will your product/service appear to be the best, fastest or cheapest?

Take the idea of selling quilting fabric by mail order as an example. To be the best, your advertising should provide details about the high-end brands of your fabrics and promise to offer the latest popular styles, colors and prints. However, if your niche is to offer the quickest service, you might stress that you always ship on the same day you receive an order. Impatient customers in the midst of a project or those far from a quilt shop would become your most likely market.

If you prefer to offer the lowest prices, you may want to become known for regular discount pricing. Your literature should stress low prices, and you might even consider offering discontinued or imperfect fabric samples.

Defining Your Product's Benefits

Whatever marketing and advertising methods you choose, your buyers must be able to perceive the benefits of your product or service to justify buying them. When customers buy a frozen dinner, for example, they settle for lower-quality food than a home-cooked meal. Convenience is what they are really buying.

Using the same theory, let's say you sell small quilted items such as place mats, totebags and wall hangings. Point out, for example, how much time customers will save when they buy from you and how distinctive handmade gifts can be.

If you hand-quilt tops for others, consider stressing a benefit this way to encourage buyers: "Do you love to appliqué but dislike hand-quilting the background? Let me do it for you, freeing you to do what you enjoy most."

Quilting teachers can gain from marketing this way as well. Your literature could say: "Do you admire beautiful handmade quilts? Do you wish you could make one yourself? Don't wait any longer. Sign up for my basic quilting class and have a lovely quilt finished by Christmas."

Compare the quoted material above to this: "I have always admired beautiful, handmade quilts. I'd like to show you how to make one. Sign up for my quilting class and I will teach you to make a quilt."

The first quote, written in the second person, addresses prospective customers and points out a clearly stated benefit: "a lovely quilt finished by Christmas." The second quote, written in the first person, has too much "I" and does not stress a benefit for the consumer.

To sum up, before spending hard-earned advertising dollars, study the results of your marketing research first.

1. Determine what you have to offer.
2. Create a clear profile of your target customer.

3. Find out how to reach them as effectively as possible.

4. Identify your product's benefits.

Tools That Speak for You: Your Image on Paper

Now that you are ready to announce to the world that you take your business seriously, create an image on paper of who you are, what you do and why you do it, making it easy for potential buyers to find you. Start with a business card. It immediately identifies you as a professional.

Business Cards

Unless you want to continually explain what "Mary's Handmade Treasures" are, make sure the name you choose clearly states what your business is. "Mary's Quilts" on the first line tells what you do. Add a subtitle such as, "Each a handmade treasure," beneath the name in a smaller font. This describes your business and states a marketing benefit: "Handmade" followed by the word "Treasure" indicates something that is of high quality and is precious enough to keep for a long time. Try to avoid cute cards not taken seriously by editors, manufacturers and other professionals.

Letterhead Stationery

Manufacturers from whom you want to buy wholesale will not consider you to be a professional or will not take you seriously if you request a catalog by writing on personal stationery or binder paper. Letterhead stationery announces that you are in business. If you have unlimited funds, you can pay a graphic artist to design both your business cards and letterhead. If you have a tight budget and access to a computer, do it yourself.

Home computers make it possible for you to select a variety of typefaces to use to design your business cards and letterhead. State your business name, your name, address, phone and fax numbers. Include Internet websites and e-mail addresses if you have these.

You need not order letterhead in bulk from a printer. Design your own letterhead, brochures, business cards and even catalogs with the help of a laser printer for a "printed" look. If you do not have a laser printer, go to a neighborhood printing company and rent one or ask the company to run as few as a dozen sheets for you on a letter-quality photocopy machine.

Brochures

Consider a brochure as your next investment. Here you can tell a more complete story about you and your business than what appears on your business cards and letterhead. If you write your own brochure text, here are a few points to keep in mind. Use an economy of words. Verbs and nouns shout a strong, easy-to-understand message. Too many adjectives and adverbs clutter your message. Use forceful but simple language stressing the benefits of your service or product. Do you need to brush up on your writing skills? Read *Thirty Days to More Powerful Writing* by Jonathan Price. This inexpensive book will help you develop a more dynamic writing style.

When designing your brochure, choose paper heavier than standard 20# bond. Simple is better, so consider a bifold brochure style. Or fold an 8½″ × 11″ sheet of paper into thirds using a standard letter fold. Hold it vertically and you have six distinct panels to organize your information in. Here is a suggested arrangement for your information, but feel free to design your own:

- **Panel #1:** The front cover should contain only your business name, your name, address and phone numbers including fax. If you have a logo, include it here also.
- **Panel #2:** Use the left inside panel to describe your product or service.
- **Panel #3:** Use the center inside panel to include a brief biographical (bio) sketch. See the next page for hints to help you prepare your bio. If you can afford it, you might consider a photo of yourself at the top of this section.
- **Panel #4:** Use the right inside panel to describe the typical customers you serve (your target market).
- **Panel #5:** Use the center outside panel for a mission statement or leave it blank if you want to address the brochure for mailing.
- **Panel #6:** Use the right outside panel to list endorsements and testimonials from satisfied customers.

Never attend professional functions, conferences or seminars without a handful of business cards and brochures. Hand them to those who ask questions about your business. Let your brochure tell your story to the recipient when he or she has more time to study your information later.

Don't forget a resume. It speaks for you too. Some experts suggest that you limit a resume to one page. If you have extensive experience and references, two pages are tops.

Your Portfolio

Buyers, editors and publishers peruse portfolios at shows, seminars and conferences. At home, shop owners, teaching centers and others interested in hiring or buying from you can also receive a professional, pictorial story about you and your business from a well-arranged, compelling portfolio.

Quilters sometimes confuse a scrapbook for a professional portfolio. Padding the cover of a binder and adding a patchwork design framed by a ruffle shouts "scrapbook." A proper, zippered portfolio portrays your business image far more professionally. Available in stationery or art supply shops, portfolios enable you to position photographs, and tearsheets from magazines featuring your designs and copies of published articles between nonslippery plastic pages. To create a professional image, take care not to crowd the pages of your portfolio by placing too many small items on one page as in a collage.

WHAT TO PUT IN YOUR PORTFOLIO

- *Your business card*, placed in the small window on the inside cover.
- *Your brochure.*
- *A short biography.* Type this on your letterhead stationery. Your bio should be a well-written statement about yourself. Try to provide answers to questions others often ask such as when, where and why you began quilting. State when and where you became a professional and close with your recent achievements.
- *Your resume.* Many new quilters worry that they don't have much professional experience to list. If you are just starting out, list your education and past work experience, especially if it relates to your present professional quilting activity (e.g., a degree in art, a sewing business and so on).
- *A photograph of yourself.* Polaroids and fuzzy snapshots do not project the image you want. Strive for professional quality in your photos or hire a photographer.
- *A mission statement.* This describes what you do, how you do it and why you care about it. Let your passion for your work shine through in just a few paragraphs written on your letterhead stationery.
- *Tear sheets from magazines.* When the designs of established quilt designers appear in magazines, the publisher sends them one or more complimentary copies in which the work appeared. Tear the page from the magazine (thus the term tear sheets). Trim ragged edges and ads or other text not related to your work. Place one tear sheet per portfolio page. Type the name, date and issue of the publication on a label and paste it neatly above the tear sheet.

If your work has not yet been published, don't despair. Try writing a letter to the editor of a magazine or newspaper, offering your opinion on a pertinent quilt-related issue. You might also write articles for newsletters of local craft groups or fraternal organizations. Even though you receive no payment for these, their appearance in your portfolio will project professional credibility.

• *Magazine covers that feature your work.* If you are fortunate enough to have your quilts appear on the cover of a magazine, position it prominently in your portfolio.

• *Articles written about you by others have great value.* Include the article labeled with the date and issue number of the magazine or newspaper in your portfolio. Writing about yourself and your work is not as effective as when someone else writes about you. The publicity adds credibility to your professional status.

• *Photos of completed quilts and related items.* Group photographs of quilts for sale and a label stating, "Available Designs," will separate these from those items no longer available. Color photos of completed projects form the heart of your portfolio, so make them as professional as possible. These can range from $3'' \times 5''$ snapshots to full-page $8'' \times 10''$ professional photos.

• *A series of color photos showing a project in progress always catches the viewer's eye.* Include several photos showing:

    a. A collection of fabrics for a quilt

    b. A shot of the quilt top before assembling the quilt sandwich

    c. The basted quilt

    d. The completed quilt on a bed or hanging on a wall

• *Photographs of your quilts displayed during shows and exhibits create credibility.* Label each to show where your work appeared with the place, date and name of the show.

• *Photographs of awards, ribbons and recognitions.* Treasure your awards, ribbons and recognitions. Don't include the actual ribbon itself for it creates too much bulk. Instead, take a close-up photo of the quilt with the ribbon attached. Add the program booklet issued at the show that details winning entries and the name, place and date of the event.

• *Copies of class schedules describing your classes if you teach.* Make sure the name of the school, shop or event appears at the top of the class description sheet.

ARRANGING YOUR PORTFOLIO

Place promotional documents like your resume, brochure, bio and mission statement in the front pages of your portfolio. Many craft designers, artists and quilters arrange remaining portfolio items in one of the three ways listed below:

    1. *Chronological.* Show photos, articles, tear sheets and so on in sequence from

front to back, starting with your earliest designs. Some people reverse the process, adding new designs to the front while keeping older work in the back.

2. *Style.* If you make traditional as well as contemporary quilts, for example, have a section for each group, placing photos of similar styles together.

3. *Technique.* If you make quilts as well as wearables, group these in separate sections. For example, you can show your quilts in one section, wearables in another and stuffed patchwork toys in a third. Take care to update your portfolio regularly. A well-prepared, organized portfolio presents a pictorial documentation and history of your quilting business. Treasure it and share it at every opportunity.

CHAPTER 3 CHECKLIST

✓ Remember that marketing never ends. Research constantly. Stay in touch with wholesalers and manufacturers to remain up-to-date on the industry. Request quilt and sewing catalogs and study them. Join quilting, sewing and craft associations. Subscribe not only to consumer quilt magazines but to trade journals as well. Attend quilting events frequently to remain as informed as possible. Marketing, a never-ending process, is critical to the success of your business.

✓ Establish and remain focused on your niche in the marketplace. When considering adding a new activity to your business time, ask yourself if it fits in with the goals outlined in your marketing plan.

✓ Never lose sight of the preferences, needs and interests of your target customer. Know where to find her. Find out what she reads so you will know where to advertise.

✓ Make the benefits of your product or service clear to consumers. Take time to describe what you can do for them in your brochures and other documents.

✓ Complete your marketing plan *before* deciding when, how and where to advertise.

✓ Project a professional image with appropriate, dynamic business cards, brochures and letterhead stationery.

✓ Take time to compile a proper portfolio. Keep it up-to-date, fresh and appealing. Let it tell your story.

DAPHNE GREIG—
QUILTER, TEACHER
AND CONSULTANT

Daphne Greig's efforts at marketing herself and her services led to her success. Early on, she understood the importance of responding to opportunities promptly and with meticulous preparation. Today she takes advantage of computers and technology like the Internet to keep her business vital and flourishing.

Daphne's entree into quilting did not happen overnight. In fact, she began very modestly. "It was my grandmother who made quilts," recalls Daphne, "but she died before she could pass her skills along to me."

Daphne remembers as a child watching a relative make a beautiful Amish Shadow quilt. This relative rewarded Daphne's interest with a special gift—her first quilting book.

"The book helped me make my first quilt for my first child in 1981," says Daphne. "I used six large squares and only two fabrics. I hand-quilted the outline of a simple fish and sailboat in every other block and felt proud of my first effort."

Daphne's quilting interest grew more serious in 1986 when she decided that her daughter's bed just didn't look right—it needed a quilt! Feeling unprepared to tackle such a large project alone, Daphne signed up for her first quilting class at a local quilt shop.

"Rotary cutters had just appeared on the market—a marvelous invention!" exclaims Daphne. "As I made my first, full-sized Rail Fence quilt, I developed a passion for anything quilted—traditional or contemporary."

Next, Daphne turned her attention to her son's bed, then to her own. "After that, I began making frequent trips to the local library, but not for novels. I discovered the quilt book shelf!"

After covering the beds in her home with quilts, Daphne made smaller projects like small quilts and wall hangings. Two friends invited Daphne to display her work at their Christmas home boutique, and these sales inspired her to try more challenging patterns.

Soon Daphne began selling her work on consignment in a local quilt shop. Attracted by her designs, the shop owner invited Daphne to teach in the shop. "I could not imagine myself as a teacher at first," confessed Daphne, "but I wanted to try. Now I'm glad because the experience was simply wonderful."

Daphne says her love of quilt trivia prompted her to read every quilting book she could find and to watch quilt shows on public television. Both activities paid off, according to Daphne. "Students loved my passing these little details and tips along to them. They told me they appreciated learning as much as possible."

In 1992, Daphne began teaching quilting part time while working at a full-time job as a data analyst. She credits the wonderful support of her family with enabling her to teach and work full time. "My husband prepared meals and both my children pitched in with the household chores," acknowledges Daphne. "I haven't touched the vacuum for years except to pick up threads in my studio occasionally."

Daphne learned to market her services promptly. For example, when a brand-new fabric shop opened nearby, Daphne acted immediately. Armed only with samples of her work and well-written class proposals, she was the first teacher who took the time to visit the shop, introducing herself to the owner. She got the job! Next, Daphne visited an out-of-town fabric shop while on vacation and inquired as to if they held classes. "I met with the owner and showed her a sample of my work and indicated an interest in teaching at her shop. This resulted in my traveling to teach several classes there as well." Together with teaching in her local shop, Daphne doubled the number of classes she offered. Like many of us, Daphne also experienced disappointment and unexpected problems.

Two days before Christmas in 1993, Daphne's husband lost much of his income due to his employer's financial problems. Daphne remembers her feelings. "Panic set in! I wondered what I could do to replace the lost income. My teaching schedule was so full, I couldn't teach any more classes. Who wanted to take classes at midnight? When would I sleep?"

Desperation soon prompted Daphne to act on impulse. She invited the owner of the shop where she did most of her teaching over for coffee. She explained her situation and asked if the store could use a seamstress. "I offered to make placemats, tea cozies or anything they made and sold in the store. The owner felt I would find that boring, then made a suggestion I couldn't refuse." The shop owner invited Daphne to make store models of quilts and wearables to help advertise the shop's new books and patterns.

Daphne agreed and explained what this opportunity came to mean for her. "Making up so many models gave me the chance to try new ideas and to experiment with tools and techniques I may not otherwise have tried," admits Daphne. "Customers responded to my handmade models by requesting new classes from me so they, too, could learn the latest quilting techniques based upon the latest patterns and quilts featured in books. I taught even more classes based on several of my store models, including patchwork clothing such as pieced vests and jackets."

While working at the shop, Daphne met a part-time employee, Susan, who also enjoyed teaching. Together they began Patchworks Studio, a business specializing in offering classes to quilters who use a computer to design quilts. Enthusiastic about designing their own quilts, the partners became experts using the software program, The Electric Quilt. They now represent the company, consulting with and helping new users of the program and selling copies of both The Electric Quilt (EQ) and its companion program, BlockBase, an electronic version of *Encyclopedia of Pieced Quilt Patterns* by quilt historian Barbara Brackman. The latter places over 3,500 blocks at the disposal of computer-literate quilters with the click of a mouse!

Along with their newest venture, a collection of five original quilt patterns with Canadian themes, Daphne and Susan market both programs by sending brochures to quilt shops throughout British Columbia. Currently, they are working to replace their old brochures by developing a new one that will highlight classes, feature their patterns and offer the latest versions of the software.

Daphne, like many crafters, created a home page on the World Wide Web. Quilters learn about what she has to offer through links from other well-known quilting sites such as Canadian Quilters Online and QuiltBiz, an American mailing list for professional quilters. Daphne has also made sure that World Wide Web search engines like Yahoo and Alta Vista refer to her site when users search for quilting information. (More information about websites on the Internet in chapter ten.)

Susan and Daphne have also developed an online Block-of-the-Month Club. Quilters who join the club receive patterns of blocks on a monthly basis. The partners design the blocks using EQ or BlockBase and provide clear instructions, suggestions for fabrics and ideas for quilt layouts using the block. "We love to share the many tips we've gathered through our own quilting experiences and research with members of our club," says Daphne.

Today Daphne teaches and quilts for many reasons. Her family enjoys the "extras" her income provides, like dining out. "My earnings enable me to pay for fabric, new tools, magazines and books without stressing our family budget. I wouldn't be able to afford all the quilt-related luxuries I want without the money I earn," she explains.

Her principal reason for teaching, however, is to share her enthusiasm, to see beginners complete their sampler quilts and to teach new skills to experienced quilters. This provides her with a great sense of satisfaction. Daphne remembers how excited she felt after mastering a new block or technique. "Today I love generating the same excitement in my students."

DAPHNE GREIG: PATCHWORKS STUDIO

903 Clayton Road, Sidney, B.C. V8L 5M3

Phone:

(250) 656-4314

E-mail:

agreig@IslandNet.com

Website:

http://www.IslandNet.com/~agreig/

WHERE TO SELL YOUR QUILTING

Quilters wanting to sell their work directly to the consumer have many alternatives from which to choose. Let's explore several opportunities.

Craft Fairs

Webster's College Dictionary defines a "craft fair" as: (1) a periodic gathering of buyers and sellers in an appointed place; (2) an exposition in which exhibitors participate, with the purpose of buying or selling or familiarizing the public with products. Who can say it better?

If you enjoy meeting the public and talking to potential buyers personally, you may enjoy working a craft fair. Think about what you hope to sell at a fair. Your answer will determine which type of fair from the list below would best suit your needs.

- *Local, neighborhood craft shows, fairs and exhibits* provide opportunities to make direct sales and to test your market with little risk and expense.
- *State, county and local general fairs* are a good choice if you offer quilted items with broad, general appeal. Here, too, you will make direct sales.
- *Quilt shows* that attract quilters at all levels may be better if you have products specifically directed at them such as tools, books and patterns. This would also allow you to make direct sales to quilt-oriented consumers.
- Consider attending *trade shows* if you prefer to sell wholesale products to retailers, who in turn will sell your product to the final customer. These become indirect sales.

Now, let's take a closer, in-depth look at each selling opportunity.

Local Shows

To learn if the fair circuit is for you, look for neighborhood shows that will rent a space for a small fee. Travel expenses are low and table and booth fees are minimal. Church fund-raisers and other nonprofit events are easy to find in your community too. Look for event names, places and dates in your local newspaper and at Chamber of Commerce offices. Call or write show sponsors to request application forms. After you work a few such shows, you will have a realistic picture of the market for your products. Street fairs, fund-raisers and privately sponsored craft shows are also worth considering to get you started.

State and County Fairs

Finished products such as bed quilts, wall hangings, toys, clothing and accessories appeal to the buying public shopping at state and county fairs. However, you may be surprised to learn that while customers prefer exclusive, one-of-a-kind handmade items, they often expect to pay the same prices as they pay for ready-mades in chain or department stores. It's up to you to educate your buyers and to explain the differences between handmade and mass-produced items.

Make sure your display information and brochures include details about your creative process. Photos of you at work and those that show works-in-progress also help tell potential buyers your story. Smile warmly while you explain the benefits of your products. Be ready to answer customers' questions about raw materials you use and product care, and be prepared to answer the question, "How long does it take you to make this?" many times a day. Finally, being able to process credit card purchases is important because fair-goers typically make impulse purchases. (More about this later in this chapter.)

Since you will be competing with established craft professionals who are on a higher level than you would usually find at local and neighborhood events, choose the best display equipment you can afford. Manufacturers of show display equipment advertise in craft trade journals, especially *The Crafts Report*. The latter publication also runs frequent articles about how to prepare and set up show displays of all sizes.

Quilt Shows

Quilt shows, fairs and exhibits differ from the events mentioned previously because at these shows, buyers have already expressed an avowed interest in quilting by merely attending a show. Competition may be stiff as most booth vendors will have products similar to yours. Presenting yourself as a professional in your field counts even more when dealing with quilt-knowledgeable buyers. Answer questions briefly but completely because quilt fair-goers frequently come to learn the latest about new materials, tools and techniques.

Information about your products and demonstrations of how to use them are vital. Successful vendors at quilt shows are often those who attract attention with interesting activities such as speed-cutting fabric, making templates and using tools. Pointing out the benefits of your product to potential buyers must remain your prime activity.

Finding quilt shows is relatively easy. Nearly all quilt magazines provide monthly listings of shows throughout the U.S. Contact show organizers to request information and application forms. (You'll find a complete magazine list, in chapter ten.) If you belong to quilt and craft guilds, you will receive advance notice about upcoming quilt shows.

Since the consumer shows just discussed offer merchandise directly to consumers, you will need to collect state sales taxes from them. (More about this in chapter six.)

Trade Shows

Trade shows also known as wholesale shows, require more preparation and professional status than the other shows described above. Here you will sell to professionals who own shops, boutiques and catalogs, and have other retail connections. They will help you create new markets for your products.

Trade shows are fewer in number than retail, consumer-oriented shows. Expect to prove you are part of the sewing or quilting trade when applying to attend or participate in these shows. Since they do not admit consumers, professionals must prove they qualify by producing any or all of the following:

- A business license from the city where you live
- Copies of your seller's permit if you plan to sell at the show
- A letter requesting show information written on letterhead stationery
- A voided business check
- A business card

Since these professionals sell your products for you, realize that when you are selling to them, you should charge wholesale prices—not retail. Customers who patronize their business will pay the retail price for your products and the shop owner will collect the sales taxes, not you.

Prepare thoroughly to deal with experienced professionals who are already experts in some aspect of the quilting market. Though you charge them less, remember that when you act as a wholesaler, you can require minimum orders to encourage larger sales. Keep in mind that unlike consumer sales, payment is not immediate. You may wait sixty to ninety days for payment from retailers.

ANNUAL TRADE SHOWS

The annual Fall International Quilt Festival and Quilt Market in Houston is the largest trade show in the country devoted exclusively to quilting. The group sponsors a smaller Spring Market, held in various parts of the country. This event offers many classes and lectures. Product information from the most prominent quilt-related manufacturers and retailers abound. Write to International Quilt Market, 7660 Woodway, Suite 550, Houston, Texas, 77063 or fax (713) 781-8182 to request information.

Consider also nonquilt-specific trade shows. The Hobby Industry Association (HIA) sponsors the largest of all the annual craft trade shows in the country. Quilt vendors sell at this show along with hundreds of other craft professionals. HIA shows are held each January, alternating sites in Las Vegas, California and Texas. See HIA's address, trade show and membership benefits in chapter nine.

TRADE SHOW BENEFITS

Feeling unsure about how a huge craft trade show like HIA's with over 28,000 booths can benefit quilters? From personal experience, let me say that you will find much of interest. Years ago, the first workshops I could find about rotary cutting and self-healing mats took place at an HIA show. Contacts I made there with the leading batting manufacturers continue to serve me well today. During a show I recently attended, I took seventeen low-fee classes at $7 each. One featured stencil painting on fabric and another featured bead decor on fabric. Within a year, I had designed and completed two quilts using the new products and techniques I learned there. Both quilt designs were published. One appeared in *Crafts*, a well-known craft magazine, and the other in *Lady's Circle Patchwork Quilts* magazine, a leading quilting publication. Both added to my income and credibility as a quilting professional. Additionally, manufacturers provided everything I needed to complete both of the quilts.

Teacher and Demonstrator Certification

HIA offers important certification programs that will train you as a certified craft teacher or craft demonstrator. Several quilters of my acquaintance, now certified demonstrators of quilt products, find that performing this service during shows pays for their travel expenses to the show. HIA's brochure cover says it all. "If craft hobbies are your business . . . anywhere in the world, HIA is the association with the tools and connections you need!" I'll vouch for that.

Start Small

Regardless of which type of show you choose, start small and work up to larger events, for you will need to gather practical experience. You must learn to:

- Set up appealing displays to showcase your products
- Greet the public, explain your wares and answer unexpected questions
- Set prices appropriately for your geographical area
- Build up an adequate inventory of goods available for sale well before an event

Key Resources

For listings of most craft shows across the country, look to *The Crafts Report*.

Another comprehensive, excellent source of American shows is the quarterly *Crafts Fair Guide*, published by Lee Spiegel. Also, check out the book, *How to Sell What You Make: The Business of Marketing Crafts at Fairs, Boutiques and Exhibits* by Paul Gerards, published by Stackpole Books. It offers much information in a simple format to help you prepare to sell at shows. See chapter ten for addresses of these publications.

Selling on Consignment

Now let's look at selling on consignment. Unlike commission work (see page 60), you must first design and complete an item, then look for a buyer. Visit local consignment shops, malls and galleries to begin your research. Survey the shop carefully to answer the following questions:

1. What items fill the shop?
2. Will your work fit in?
3. Does your style fit the shop's mood, theme and price range?
4. Does the staff respect the work of its consignors, protecting it from customer handling?

5. Do you find most items tastefully displayed?

Don't overlook craft malls, another popular consignment method of selling. Crafter's malls continue to grow at a phenomenal rate across the country. Some require you to sell your wares in person. Others have a co-op system where someone else sells your items directly to the consumer. Visit those nearby and check out the competition. If you cannot find a crafter's mall nearby, lists of them across the country appear in trade journals and on the Internet. Write to ask if you can deal with them at a distance as you do with out-of-state consignment shops. Check the popular Coomer's Craft Malls on the World Wide Web. (See chapter ten for the address.)

Consignment Contracts

Once you find a shop or craft mall with whom you'd like to work, express interest and ask to see their consignment contract. Shop owners always protect their own interests in their contracts, but the contracts do not always protect the interests of the individual consignor. Here are a few key areas to investigate:

DISPLAY

How will they display your work? If you submit a full-sized quilt, for example, will it hang on a wall or rest on a bed? If it's the latter, will customers be able to sit on the quilt or handle it? Does the shop allow customers to bring food and drinks into the shop? Quilts fade in direct sunlight. Request that your work be protected from this as well as overhandling by many caressing hands.

PERCENTAGE AGREEMENT

What percentage of the retail price goes to the shop owner and to you? Though amounts vary from one shop to another, the last few years show that 50/50 is becoming the normal division, though you will still find some that pay 60/40 or even 70/30, with the larger amount going to the consignor. *Never* settle for an oral agreement here; get it in writing.

PRICING

Does the shop owner have the right to lower your retail price if the quilt does not sell in a given time? If you don't want this to happen, say so in writing. At times, experienced shop owners realize a quilt is underpriced and would bring in more money if the price were higher than the one you set. If you disapprove of this, again, say so in your contract. But if you are just starting out in consigning, take time to listen to an experienced shop or gallery owner. If you find you continually undervalue your work, your pricing schedule needs immediate attention.

NOTIFICATION TO BUYER

How long will it take the shop owner to notify you that you have a buyer for your quilt? If you did not know about the sale and the shop owner did not feel obligated to call you immediately, receiving payment for your item could take several weeks. Don't let shop owners operate on your money interest-free indefinitely. Frequently visit the shop unannounced. If the shop contract does not set a limit on when to notify you of a sale, ask to include this information in their contract. Disappointment and frustration ensue if you find that a quilt sold immediately upon display and you weren't notified.

INSURANCE

Make sure to ask if the shop has insurance that will cover your quilt while it is in their possession. A mere ''yes'' does not satisfy me. Request to see the policy or ask for the name of the insurance carrier and local agent. Fire, theft or other damage to handmade quilts may be infrequent, but when it occurs, it is always tragic. Protect yourself from this possibility by making sure that the shop owner's coverage protects your items. Talk to your own insurance agent before problems arise. Fortunately, my very competent agent introduced me and my students to the nuances of ''fine art floaters'' added to a basic homeowner's or renter's policy. He also recommended umbrella policy coverage under certain circumstances. Either of these arrangements provides coverage if your handmade items are lost or damaged under any circumstances, including while on display, in transit to another location or in your vehicle.

Check the consignee's contract for details about all of the consignment issues discussed above. As consignor, if you find that your interests are not covered to your satisfaction, either ask the consignee to amend their contract or submit your own as you negotiate further.

Expanding Your Consignment Business

Once your quilts or other handmade items saturate nearby consignment stores and are selling well, it may be time to expand. *The Crafts Report*, among other trade journals, provides monthly lists of consignment shops throughout the U.S. that are seeking textiles and quilted items. Contact them with persuasive cover letters and quality photos of your work. Good relationships with a few consignment shops across the country can keep you in business for years.

Sales Representatives Can Create Markets for You

Sales representatives offer yet another possibility for selling your quilts and related items. They advertise in craft trade journals when they wish to take on new artisans to expand their line. Hardworking reps take your items on the road for you. They find new markets at further distances than you would normally travel. They visit boutiques, shops and other retail outlets, representing you and your work. Since they usually represent several crafters, make sure your rep does not carry a competing line. For a percentage of the retail price, averaging about 15 to 20 percent, reps sell your goods outright or take custom orders on your behalf.

Carefully choose and then nurture successful business relationships once you find your reps. Competent reps can expand your market and enlarge your customer base. They can pass valuable marketing information along to you such as color and style preferences, new product ideas or price changes. Before hiring a rep, ask for a generous sampling of present clients. Then call these clients and inquire about the rep's effectiveness in finding new business and promptness with paperwork. Most importantly, ask about the condition of unsold merchandise that is returned to them. Is it still fit to resell?

Working on Commission

In addition to placing your work in consignment shops or galleries, you may also work on commission. Quilting on commission means you have a sure sale *before* you begin a new project—a happy arrangement. You don't have to worry about finding a buyer or marketing the product because in commission work, a ready buyer awaits. You will create a project made-to-order following the customer's preferences. "Customer" not only means individuals who pay you to make something for them, but also magazine publishers, manufacturers or others who commission you to make a specific project to order.

Commission Contracts

Take the time to formulate a contract to guard against misunderstandings between you and your clients when designing and/or making quilts and related items on commission. Outline the conditions under which you will work. For example, a frequent problem with quilting on commission occurs when clients change their minds or back out of an oral arrangement after you have begun their project. Avoid getting stuck with supplies ordered for a customer by requesting a down payment to cover initial purchases of raw materials *before* you shop. This prevents you from investing your money rather than the customer's.

GETTING PAID

When working on commission, never release a completed item until the customer has paid you in full. Pleading for payment you have already earned creates uncomfortable confrontations and undermines your self-esteem. Surrendering the completed item before receiving final payment also causes you to lose a valuable negotiating position.

FINDING COMMISSIONS

Use promotional methods to find clients. Write on letterhead stationery to fabric and craft shops, for example. Many keep a file of dressmakers and quilters who will work on commission. Quilt shops often have their own staff to work for customers, thus they may not be your best bet.

Place want ads in the "Services Available" section of your local newspaper or in the classified sections of quilting magazines. Contact local community groups and offer to give programs, exhibits or demonstrations about what you can do. Show your work at exhibits and fairs so others can see you at work. Onlookers at fairs or those who attend programs you present can become potential clients, so engage them in conversation. Educate them about the value of handwork, and distribute flyers and brochures describing your services whenever possible.

Selling by Mail Order

Mail-order selling enables you to offer your goods and services directly to the customers without a middleman. This method of selling continues to attract new entrepreneurs who believe that selling by mail guarantees a million-dollar income for minimum, easy work. Unfortunately, such hyperbole does not present a realistic picture. Selling by mail, however, does provide you with extra income if you are detail-minded and a diligent worker.

What to Sell

Items not readily available in retail stores, such as hand-embellished wearables and unusual, original designs, sell best. Sell not only handmade quilted items but consider patterns, kits and booklets too.

As you think about mail order, realize that you will order raw materials at wholesale prices, and sell finished items to consumers at retail prices. Even if you already have a profitable quilting business, you can consider mail-order selling as an additional form of retail sales.

Profile Your Typical Buyer

You can avoid wasting time and money if you do meticulous marketing and research before you begin. Start by writing a detailed profile of your typical buyer. Is gender or age an issue? Where do your customers live? What do you think they read? How much discretionary income do they need to be able to buy from you? If you are wondering how to learn this information, read on. (Also refer to chapter three for detailed guidelines on profiling your potential customers.) When you have defined your target mail-order customer, begin your research.

Find your typical consumer by choosing several consumer publications you believe they would read. *Quilter's Newsletter* magazine offers a large, general classified listing of fabrics, patterns, books and notions. However, *Piecework* magazine specializes in the historical aspects of quilting and might be more suitable if you wish to sell antique tools, books or patterns.

Write to the magazines to request press or media kits. You can find the magazine addresses inside on the masthead. The publications will send you everything you need to know about advertising within their pages. They will also describe their typical readers for you. When you receive the material, determine if their demographics match your customer profile. If not, contact a few other publications until your target customer coincides with the profile of the magazine's typical reader.

Next, ask yourself if your product matches what you've learned about the reader-ship. Do this by scanning the magazine's classified ads in several issues. Do you find items similar to yours listed? Select two or three magazines that closely describe your target consumer. For example, if you want to sell patterns using variations of time-honored designs, place an inexpensive ad in *Traditional Quilter* because they specialize in these. But choose *Craft Magazine* if you have innovative patterns that combine painted stencils with beads and trims. Demographics provided by both of these publications supplied the information above.

Advertising

Choose either a one- or two-step advertising process. One-step advertising means you sell your item directly to the buyer from an ad. The consumer reads your ad and sends you a check. You send the ordered product. Each of you had to take only one step to complete the sale.

Two-step advertising may be needed if your product description requires more than what you can express in a classified ad. If you need to offer potential customers a catalog or brochure providing them with more details, you have set up two-step advertising. The customer responds to your ad by requesting more information. You send a direct-mail package including a catalog, persuasive sales letter, order form and complete, detailed descriptions of the product(s). The customer sends you a check and orders the item(s). You fill and send the order. In this case, both of you had two steps to follow to complete the sale.

Complying With FTC Regulations

Contact the Federal Trade Commission (FTC) and request their free booklet explaining the mail-order rule. The FTC regulates what you may and may not sell via mail order. The booklet will help you learn how to abide by the law while satisfying your mail-order buyers. (See chapter ten for the FTC address.)

Direct-Mail Advertising

Direct-mail advertising differs from mail-order selling where potential customers read your ad and send you a check for their purchase. Direct-mail advertising means that you make your offer to consumers by sending them a catalog and other information. Success in mail order comes from repeat sales and satisfied customers. Take the time to carefully study direct-mail methods for it entails much preparation to target consumers wisely.

You can begin your own direct mail program by formulating a "house list." This means that you make a list of potential customers by using the names of your friends, neighbors and business associates. Take care to use current addresses, avoid duplications and organize the list by zip code. Continue to expand your house list by adding the name and address of everyone who sends you an order or makes an inquiry by mail. Consider also trading customer lists with other quilt-related business contacts you may have. This, too, will expand your house list.

Mailing list brokers found in the yellow pages can also help to expand your list. Brokers can create a larger list for you guided by the description of your target customer. A critical fact you must keep in mind about dealing with list brokers is that they only *rent* you their list, they do not *sell* it to you. This means you may send mailings from a list provided by a broker only *once*. Though you may add any buyers or inquirers to your house list, you may not mail to the broker's list again without paying another rental fee. List brokers make sure that those who rent their list use it only once by including a "dummy" name in the list. When your literature reaches this name a second time, you will hear from the broker that you have violated their one-time-use only rental agreement. You may rent such lists from a list broker for $70 to $90 per one thousand names, or even higher if you request specific demographics, for example, if you ask for a list of only those buyers who have purchased quilts before, are of a certain age or income, or are residents of a certain county or state.

Famous catalog houses such as Lillian Vernon, Quill Office Products and Land's End began their businesses by using direct mail. They worked from home, sending only two- or three-page catalogs at first. And so can you!

Using Established Catalogs

Consider placing your item(s) in established catalogs. Study many craft, sewing and quilting catalogs before choosing the one most suited to your product(s) and style. (A list of quilt and related catalogs appears in chapter ten.) A marketing expert in my local business network advised that anyone interested in selling by mail order should request and study every catalog they can get their hands on. Educate yourself about the varieties of sizes, styles, colors, typefaces, paper, description styles, order form formats and more.

Contact catalog companies whose product line lines up with your products. Write to them expressing your interest in having them carry your product(s). Make sure the photos you send are of professional quality. Include brochures and other literature describing your items.

When you hear from interested catalogers, prepare to negotiate. State your terms to the buyer clearly. Let the buyer know how much profit you need to compete in the marketplace. Make it clear you are willing to compromise but not surrender wholly to the catalog buyer's business preferences. You must also make your production schedule clear. No established cataloger will want to continue working with you if they advertise and receive orders for your product, only to find you cannot meet their customers' demands. If you can only make two dozen patchwork pillows per month, for example, explain this to the catalog buyer early. Later, if your pillows sell well, they have the opportunity to ask for a greater quantity while giving you sufficient time to find someone to help you produce more in less time.

Many excellent craft catalogs have editorial boards that jury potential merchandise from freelance crafters. This assures the buying public that they will receive the highest quality in handcrafted items. Consider small, specialized catalogs too. They advertise in trade journals and in various arts and crafts publications.

Learn about the needs of the mail-order company you want to work with. Many new business owners assume that mail-order catalog companies will undertake the preparation details of your item. But do not expect them to take the time to create, lay out and write your sales copy, for example. Make it easy for them to work with you by doing a good job of this yourself. Send high-quality sketches or photographs that clearly illustrate your item, and include details about prices, sizes, colors and so on. Creative people often have introverted personalities and dislike asserting themselves this way. However, if you want to profit from your craft, you must have your own business ethic. This means that you must learn assertive marketing and sales techniques, and must speak and write in a confident manner if you want to expand your business via mail order in established catalogs.

Producing Your Own Catalog

Producing a catalog alone can be expensive when you consider photography, production, printing, binding and postage, to mention a few prime expenses. Perhaps you have friends who wish to sell by mail order with whom you can share expenses and work. Do you belong to a quilt guild where several members have something to sell by mail order? Consider a co-op catalog featuring the work of each person. Several quilters pooling resources make this idea practical.

Consider placing a small ad in a networking publication and offer to trade your house mailing list of customers with another craft professional. Choose a complementary, not a competitive market. Trading lists, name-for-name, works well if you check to make sure the business you are considering has an updated list as current as yours.

HOW TO DEFRAY COSTS

Defray your own expenses by offering to include literature and brochures from colleagues in your own mailings. Suggest they do the same for you. All of you will increase the size of your in-house mailing list for little cost, reaching the consumer directly.

Help From Technology

Since this is the computer age, think about choosing computer software to facilitate your bookkeeping. Selling by mail order requires most of the basic components of computer technology.

- You need a word processing system to use for writing your ad copy, dealing with correspondence and writing instructions.
- You need a spreadsheet program to show income and expenses so your tax expert can prepare your federal income tax returns each year.
- You will need a database to maintain your customer and mailing lists.
- Eventually, you will need software enabling you to print labels although you can postpone this until your mail-order business increases.

If you decide to sell by mail order, the software you select to manage your database and make your labels is important. Consider the benefits of Mail Order Wizard to manage your business, My Advanced Mailing Labels to make labels and FileMaker Pro to set up your database. These are only suggestions. You must ask questions *before* you buy software, making sure it is both affordable and will perform as you want. See chapter ten for books about selling by mail order.

Obtaining Merchant Credit Card Status

Quilt professionals agree that accepting credit card sales from customers increases sales. However, if you work from home without a storefront, you may find it extremely difficult to obtain merchant status from a bank enabling you to accept Visa or Master-Card from your customers.

I recently invited our local banker plus the merchant credit sales representative for banks in the San Francisco Bay Area to visit my classes. I asked them to explain why obtaining merchant credit card status is so difficult for home-based workers. They explained that banks feel that storefront businesses are more stable than home-based businesses. With the acceleration and acceptance of home-based businesses across the country, this attitude is slowly changing. When you apply for merchant credit card status, your banker will ask to see:

- Income tax returns
- Credit references from vendors and distributors
- References from other banks where you have accounts
- A business plan (see chapter five)
- Statements showing how sales will increase if customers can use credit cards
- Information about the legal structure of your business
- Copies of your business license and seller's permit
- Fictitious name forms
- Zoning variances
- Yellow page advertisments
- Proof of business checking account

Also, if you take the home office deduction, a bank officer will probably come to check your home office for IRS compliance. So make sure your quilting business complies with local and state business regulations *before* you apply for credit card status.

Bankers need this information to determine whether you will be a good credit risk for them. Disputes or nonpayments left by a company that goes out of business can become the bank's responsibility, something banks want to avoid at all costs. This, our banker explained, is the reason banks want to make sure that you can prove your stability, good credit and payment history and permanence in the community.

Contact Small Local Banks

You may have to visit several banks before persuading one to grant you merchant credit. Choose smaller local banks as opposed to large, nationally known banks. Smaller institutions often display more eagerness to increase their business.

Though I knew how difficult it was for home-based businesses to gain merchant credit card status, I began the process for my needlework/quilting business five years ago. Seven banks rejected me, but much to my surprise, a small local bank accepted my application. Much of the credit goes to the bank manager, who proved how valuable a good relationship with your banker can be for a small business person. She helped and supported me once she understood my needs. She guided me and made suggestions along the way. She advocated for me as needed with the bank's head office. She explained that since I had been in business for many years and advertised in the phone book, the bank, having checked each credit and personal reference I provided, viewed my business as "stable." Most of all, she encouraged me every step along the way, explaining that she wanted my business even though it was small. She proved that her bank sincerely wanted to help clients with their businesses.

Separate Checking Accounts

If you succeed in obtaining merchant credit, you will need to open another checking account at your bank in which to deposit slips verifying your credit card sales. Each month you will receive a statement totaling your sales. It will also tell you the total percentage of each sale that is retained by your bank for the privilege of accepting credit cards.

You can choose from several different credit card authorization formats available from banks granting merchant credit card status. The two used most often by small businesses are terminal systems and Touch-Tone 1-800 phone numbers. Another method growing in popularity makes use of your personal computer to report directly to the bank. Most banks want you to wait to apply for merchant credit until you have been in business for at least one year. If the bank grants this privilege, don't be surprised to learn they want *all* of your business. They usually encourage you to strengthen your relationship with them by opening checking, savings and other accounts.

If many banks refuse you in spite of your best efforts, take heart. You have other alternatives. Since the problems home-based businesses have with obtaining merchant credit are well known, new enterprises have sprung up to meet the need. Such agencies will secure merchant credit for you, acting as brokers. Their services may cost more than banks because they charge for each service they provide. Expect to pay separately for:

- Monthly statements
- Initiation fees
- Each check processed
- Equipment rental

Contact the National Association of Credit Card Merchants, 217 N. Seacrest Boulvard, Boynton Beach, FL 33425 to request a list of approved companies who offer these services.

CHAPTER 4 CHECKLIST

✓ Though you may think fairs and exhibits are your only alternatives for direct sales, you have many other choices, such as selling by commission, consignment or mail order.

✓ Wholesale shows differ from retail shows. Which is best for your product or service? After reading about Margie Bevis, whose profile follows, you may decide to sell at both retail and wholesale shows.

✓ Whether you are selling on consignment or commission, be professional and insist on written contracts. Focus on the issues that benefit you professionally and help you to increase sales.

✓ Consider expanding your business by selling to out-of-state consignment shops. You can find regular lists of them in *The Crafts Report*.

✓ Mail-order selling can be effective and profitable but requires meticulous attention to detail and hard work. Look before you leap. Though it offers potential income, it requires extensive market research and education in the nuances of mail-order selling.

✓ Accepting credit cards from your customers is much harder than you may think.

✓ If banks reject your application, look to other agencies for help.

MARJORIE LEE BEVIS—
FABRIC MARBLING
ARTIST

Marjorie (Margie) Bevis has made a successful quilting career selling at both retail and wholesale craft shows across the country. Margie creates her unique and dazzling marbled fabrics at home and then takes them to consumer and trade shows where prospective buyers can see them. Seeing Margie's wide array of custom marbled fabrics makes them irresistible to anyone who loves fabric. Marbled designs are all originals since no two can be exactly alike. Such variety inspires Margie to spend most of her time manufacturing marbled fabric for quilters.

"I began dyeing fabric because I couldn't find all the colors I wanted to use in my quilts," says Margie. "During a dyeing class I took, we experimented with marbling for one day. For me, that was it. I've continued making quilts since, but I've never stopped marbling. I started my part-time business in 1986 as an extension of my quiltmaking."

Margie had a full-time job away from home and was busy raising two children on her own. Yet she spent twenty-five to thirty hours a week dyeing fabric and marbling. Her first professional move was to rent booth space at quilt shows to sell her fabric. "Before long," explains Margie, "I found myself spending increasing hours in my studio designing and marbling more fabric. After four and a half years of juggling both my outside job and home business, I quit my job and founded my business, Marbled Fabric & Accessories."

Today, Margie affirms she never spends less than thirty hours a week marbling. During busy times, she spend as much as ninety hours per week dyeing, marbling and packaging fabric. During such busy times, she now hires outside help to prepare the fabrics for dyeing and to iron finished marbled fabric.

Margie describes her usual workday. "My days vary depending upon which part of the process I'm doing. When marbling, I spend most of my day in my studio with the fabric. I stop only to run errands or cook dinner. After dinner, I either continue marbling or wash and iron the fabric I've painted that day. Dyeing fabric allows me a little free time. While the fabric is dyeing, I can mix paints, clean up my studio, prepare fabrics with alum or sew."

Margie continues. "Before I began my marbled fabric business, I made quilts and wall hangings for clients. I realized very quickly that I would never be able to make enough quilts to support myself and my children, so I diminished my quilting time in favor of dyeing and marbling, which is much more profitable."

Fond though she is about quiltmaking, Margie acknowledges that marbling is truly her favorite. "I often find myself thinking how lucky I am to be doing something that I love," says Margie.

Working at quilt shows four to six times per year currently takes about 25 percent of Margie's time. Creating custom designs for manufacturers who use her fabric consumes another 25 percent. Marbling fabric for wholesale shops and other fabric distributors takes the remaining time. Margie works hard to squeeze in teaching and writing instructions for students who want to learn to marble.

"Creative freedom is what I enjoy most," says Margie of her career. "Creating new patterns and colors provides endless satisfaction. Not adhering to anyone else's schedule or rules gives me a feeling of freedom. Having the sole responsibility for managing my business intrigues me.

"Dyeing and marbling suits my personality. I am independent, work hard and don't like living with someone else's rules with which I may not agree. Supporting my family with my small business continues to challenge me. My ability to work hard and long hours if necessary, and my desire to continually create new patterns and products are my strengths. Bookkeeping and marketing activities are definitely weak areas for me."

71

Margie states her long-range goals clearly. "I plan to supply more quilt shops and manufacturers with beautiful, one-of-a-kind fabrics. Another of my long-term goals is to write a book containing descriptions of how to marble along with beautiful examples of marbled silk and cotton fabrics."

Like many crafters, Margie reads to remain informed. She admits she reads *all* of the quilt magazines. "I look to see who has used my fabric and how they utilized it. *Art News Magazine* inspires me."

Margie's heartfelt advice to others is, "Choose a part of the quilting industry you love dearly because you will spend a lot of time with it. Research your market. Learn who will buy your product and always keep trying to develop something new."

MARGIE BEVIS: MARBLED FABRIC & ACCESSORIES

325 4th Street, Petaluma, CA 94952

Phone:

(707) 762-7514

E-mail:

marblefab@aol.com

WHEN YOUR HOBBY BECOMES A BUSINESS

Crafters of all types who are enrolled in my small business college classes express a common problem as they turn professional. Business matters, especially bookkeeping, receive too little of their attention because as creative people, they value their artistic interests more. They often continue to think like a hobbyist rather than a business owner when entering the marketplace. Such thinking challenges them as they make a transition from hobby to a for-profit enterprise. The IRS *requires* you to maintain your books and records following business standards common today.

Novice entrepreneurs say they fear compromising their creative ethic when actively marketing their products. Quilters can resent the time spent on bookkeeping or correspondence tasks. Their hearts yearn for what they perceive as "real work." They want to spend all of their time with their hands on needle and fabric instead.

However, the very business activities we shun are those we must develop if we want our quilting to become profitable enough to earn a living or supplement existing incomes. Undoubtedly, most feel that bookkeeping is not as much "fun" as creating designs or hand-quilting. Yet we must discipline ourselves to learn all we can about accounting, advertising and marketing if we want to profit from our artistic talents.

How to Tell When Your Hobby Becomes a Business

If you have been considering turning your quilting hobby into a business, you may wonder how to tell when the time is right to get started. Here are four guideposts to help you recognize when your quilting hobby may be turning into a business. If you:

- Began only to Make Your Quilting Pay for Itself, but have found that your income also extends to pay living or other expenses, a business may be in the works.

- Find yourself increasing quilting time to work for others and setting your own projects aside, your quilting activities may be more business than hobby.

- Find yourself keeping notes or an informal bookkeeping system to track expenses and income, you've begun a business process.

- Make more than $400 per year from your quilting. The Internal Revenue Service statutes say that when a taxpayer *nets* more than $400 per year, she must file a Schedule C with her income tax return to report self-employed income. When a small business shows a profit—that is to say, you have made money (or your deductions plus expenses are less than your income) for three out of five years—a viable enterprise exists.

What Next?

If your quilting activities show a profit and you see a small business emerging, you have a few decisions to make. Begin by assessing the time you will need to spend developing your business. Is it feasible to add more quilting time to your present work-at-home schedule?

Incorporating a new pursuit into your life requires adjustment. If you feel drawn to do so, consider your work style and personality next, as you explore the possibility of creating a business. Many people express the need to work around others, to give and receive regular feedback about group interests. Does this describe you? If so, you may want to rethink starting your business at home, for you will work in solitude much of the time. While many creative people enjoy working alone, others deplore it. Does the new lifestyle suit you? If you have answered "yes" to the previous questions and still feel determined to explore converting your quilt hobby to a small business, consider what the IRS has to say.

You and the IRS

The IRS is the definitive guide about tax issues and deductions that affect your business. The IRS requires your craft business to show a clear "profit motive." This means you must make every effort to make a profit and to pay taxes on the income you earn.

Give your new quilt enterprise the respect it deserves. Prepare. To turn your hobby into a business and prove that you aim to make a profit, you must:

- Maintain a general business ledger to document all deductible expenses and income. You may use very expensive systems but a small, inexpensive ledger will satisfy the IRS. Computer-generated spreadsheets are acceptable too.
- Keep invoices and receipts in good order to affirm your expenses and income.
- Make regular business transactions.
- Set aside time devoted to your business.
- Prove general business practices such as advertising, bank accounts, legal licenses and permits and a business name.
- Show a profit three out of five years or present solid evidence of your effort to do so.

When the IRS finds your business shows a profit, you have no problem identifying your activities as "business." However, the IRS can declare your business as a "hobby," an activity not engaged in for profit, if you do not follow general business practices.

Small business owners can deduct business losses but "hobbies" cannot. Remember that even if you list your quilting activities as a hobby, if you generate income from them, you must still add a Schedule C to your annual returns and pay taxes on the earnings. While business owners can deduct losses, hobbyists can only deduct expenses equal to the amount of income generated.

The IRS office offers many free booklets to help you establish a profitable business.

Getting Legal: Licenses and Permits

When the time arrives to switch your quilting activities from a hobby to a business, here are four legal issues to consider.

A Name for Your Business

Choosing a name is the first step to starting your business. This is more complicated than it sounds. Legally, you *must* include your *full* name in the business title *or* file a fictitious name form at your county clerk's office. You may not call your business "Betty's Quilts" or "Bell's Quilts" because this does not completely identify you. If you want to use one of the two examples above, you must still file a fictitious name form. You *may* call your business "Betty Bell's Beauteous Quilts" because the title includes both your first and last name and thus would not require you to file the form.

Full disclosure about who owns your business, its location and the legal form of your business (proprietorship, partnership or corporation) must become public information so people in your community can find you readily. If you need help deciding which legal form of business is best for you, see chapter ten on how to contact the IRS and request their free literature comparing the advantages of each. You will find this information in books about small businesses also listed in chapter ten.

After you file a fictitious name form, you also must publish the information it contains in a county newspaper in four consecutive issues. Your information becomes a part of the public business record in your county. If you use your full legal name as the name of your business, you will not need to file a fictitious name form. You also do not need to publish your business information in a newspaper because your business name, which is also your legal name, will become public knowledge, enabling anyone who needs to find you to do so easily.

You may not select a name already in use by someone else in your county, though you may use a name registered elsewhere if it is not trademarked. Check existing records in your county clerk's office and prepare ahead of time by having alternative business names in mind. If you find another business exists in your county using your first choice, you can quickly submit the next name on your list without wasting time returning home to choose another.

Filing fees to register names are small. Renewal is required every five years, though this varies from state to state. You may choose the same name used by a business in a neighboring county or state. Thus, we have many "Quilter's Corners" and "Quilter's Attics" across the country.

Trademarking your business name is the only way to assure exclusive ownership in the U.S. Contact the U.S. Patent Office in Washington, DC, for their free trademark literature. Begin the process by completing an application form. Later you will need to pay a $280 registration fee. A trademark search will be made to determine if the name you have chosen is already in use. If so, you must select another. Remember, all of the above is unnecessary if your business name contains your first and last name.

City Business License

City hall is your next stop if you live in an incorporated city. Cities charge a fee for a business license, which permits you to generate income within city limits. While a few cities across the U.S. do not license home-based workers, most do. Call your city hall for information since rates vary widely. If you live outside the city limits, you may find that your county requires a county business license. Check your city and county business offices to make sure you know what they require.

Those of you who plan to work from home may feel discouraged to learn that not all cities welcome home-based businesses and may refuse to license them. Though this policy is changing across the country due to the growth of home-based businesses, resistance still occurs. Your city may insist you operate your new business from a downtown site. Homeowner associations may be sticky to deal with too. Did you sign an agreement when you rented or bought your condo that you would not use the premises to conduct a business?

Home Occupation Use Permits

Across the country, local city and county governments have recently come to recognize the great increase in home-based businesses. Often they conclude that this national trend can generate additional tax revenues. Thus, many but not all cities have instituted the home occupation use permit. This permit is separate and in addition to a city business license. Cities describe this as a tax levied against home-based workers, granting them permission to generate an income from home. This tax has created great resentment and controversy but is one you must know about. Contact your city hall to learn whether or not you must pay this tax.

Residential Zoning Variance

You *may* need a zoning variance. Most homes within city limits are zoned for residential use only. Business districts receive commercial zoning. When you conduct a business from your home, most cities require that you apply for and perhaps pay for a variance to alter the zoning. There may be a one-time fee. Call your planning commission to determine your zoning status and the cost of obtaining a variance. Bear in mind that cities (and your neighbors) want home-based businesses to be unobtrusive, invisible and otherwise not detrimental to the neighborhood.

The Home Office Deduction

The IRS allows owners of small, home-based businesses to write off a portion of their home mortgage payment or rental as a business deduction. This frequently misunderstood deduction adds profit to a home-based business. Taxpayers often fear it, not understanding this important tax advantage. Home business owners assume this deduction triggers an IRS audit more than any other issue. Not true! Random selection targets the most tax audits. The home office deduction ranks fifth as a reason for selecting taxpayers for audits according to most certified public accountants. Major repairs, alterations, modifications and furnishing expenses for your home office are 100 percent deductible, but always check with your tax professional and make sure.

How the Home Office Deduction Works

The IRS allows home-based workers to deduct a percentage of their rent or mortgage interest payments, utilities (except for the phone) and real estate taxes as business expenses. These deductions lower your annual gross income, which in turn lowers the amount of annual taxes you pay. The vital aspect of this deduction is that you must use the room or space in which you work *exclusively* for your business. Setting up your sewing machine on the dining room table does *not* qualify the area as a legitimate home office. Remove all furniture and personal items that the IRS perceives as non-business-related.

The home office deduction also requires you to use your home as your business headquarters. If you have a business telephone in your home, receive business mail there and meet clients and customers, you qualify. You should not have any problems if your home is the *primary* location of the business and you spend most of your working hours there. Note that you do not have to spend *all* of your time at home. Think of home-based gardeners and housekeepers for example. While they operate their businesses from home, they must leave it to work. Note that all business-related trips from your home by car also generate a mileage deduction. More about this later in this chapter.

Other Deductions You Should Know About

Successful home-based business owners realize that being meticulous about taking every deduction to which they are entitled lowers the tax they must pay. Here is a list of common deductions:

1. Office and studio equipment and supplies
2. Postage and freight charges
3. Marketing and advertising fees
4. Licenses
5. Separate insurance for your business such as "fine arts floaters"

6. Photography costs associated with magazines, craft shows, fairs and exhibits to promote your quilting

7. Entrance fees and booth rentals for shows, fairs and exhibits

8. Automobile mileage—keep a notebook in your car to note every trip to the post office, bank, wholesalers and any other trip that is business-related.

9. Visual aids including materials for making samples and display items and for teaching and demonstrating your quilting

10. Continuing education including courses, workshops and books you need to stay on top of your particular industry. When traveling away from home to attend national seminars, document expenses carefully. Such deductions put money in your pocket when you fastidiously record and document them with invoices and receipts.

11. Dues and subscriptions to professional groups, magazines and journals to remain informed about the industry.

12. Wages you pay to anyone who works for you part or full time

13. Fees paid to consultants such as attorneys, tax preparers, graphic artists and business advisors

14. Telephones. If you have only a personal phone in your home, you may only deduct long-distance calls. To deduct your monthly phone bill together with phone services such as call-waiting, you must install a second business-only phone line. A mere extension of your personal phone line does not qualify. You must install a second line with a separate number. Once you have the second number, that is used exclusively for business, all phone expenses become a deduction including installation fees, the phone itself and your monthly payment.

Quilters working from home generally qualify for the home office deduction, but consult your tax professional for specifics about your situation. Call the IRS office and request their *free* pamphlet, *Business Use of Your Home* (#587), to decide whether or not this valuable deduction suits your business and your home.

Buying Wholesale

One of the steps in becoming a quilt professional is to begin buying raw materials your business requires at wholesale prices. Absolutely *never* run your business by purchasing raw materials on sale from a retailer. Hobbyists do that. Professional quilters find distributors and/or wholesalers to buy supplies in larger quantities at prices greatly reduced from retail.

Visit your county's State Board of Equalization office to obtain a seller's permit. This document enables you to buy products at wholesale prices in order to sell them at retail to consumers. In addition to allowing you to purchase wholesale items for resale in your business, permits are often required as admission to trade shows that consumers cannot attend. Your permit number identifies you as a business interested in buying. Minor differences exist from state to state, so check the uses and limitations of permits in your area.

Misconception #1

The idea of buying quilt supplies at wholesale prices excites new business owners. They envision buying countless items they have always wanted at greatly reduced prices. However, this is a misconception. A seller's permit, also known as a "resale license," "wholesale license" or a "buyer's permit," enables you to buy at wholesale prices only what you will resell to the ultimate consumer—the person who takes the item home. This does not include office supplies, sewing machines or other tools used to produce your quilts. These items are for business use, not for resale.

After you receive your permit, you will be required to collect state sales taxes on every retail dollar earned from the direct sale of products. The amount of sales tax varies from state to state. Each State Board of Equalization office provides free information about the amount of sales taxes to collect in each of its counties. Think of yourself as a volunteer tax collector for the state.

Plan to keep sufficient funds on hand so you can pay your sales taxes promptly to avoid penalties. Your State Board of Equalization will determine if you must pay your sales taxes annually or quarterly based upon your anticipated gross income.

Misconception #2

The second misconception about a seller's permit is that business owners just starting out assume that having the permit assures them that all wholesalers will want to sell to them. This may not always be true. If, for example, a nearby shop has a contract with a wholesaler for exclusive selling privileges, the wholesaler will usually be loyal to the established company and exclude you as a new buyer.

Some wholesale vendors guard against selling to buyers who just want the lowest prices for personal use, so they set their minimum orders so high that a home-based quilting business cannot afford to buy.

Tips to Help You Contact Prospective Wholesalers

To avoid sounding like a hobbyist, make your application letter brief, business-like and to the point. Always write on letterhead stationery to indicate your professional status. Let them know you are familiar with their product line and explain how you will use their merchandise. Ask about "terms of sale," which means you want information about minimum order amounts and preferred methods of payment. Study their terms carefully. Profit interests vendors most. Persuade them that you will increase their business and tell them the ways their company will benefit from dealing with you. Tell them if your plans will include a steady stream of orders. Convince them that you are serious about your business.

Wholesale Business Practices

Business practices vary from one vendor to another. While some require high minimum orders, others sell one item at a time. Some permit you to buy COD and others will allow you to place orders by credit card. Prepare for a few inevitable refusals by contacting more distributors than you need. This way you can still choose from those that offer to deal with you.

The *Craft Supply Directory* targets professional crafters of all types. It includes ads from companies who sell to home-based individuals and host conventions and seminars geared to the nonshop craft professional. See chapter ten for the address.

Refer to *The Thomas Register* in your library, which lists all American manufacturers and wholesalers. Search by subject matter or company name. Here you will find everything manufactured in the U.S. from adhesives to zippers. *The Thomas Register* is *the* most comprehensive listing of wholesalers anywhere. You may also purchase it on a CD for your computer, or research their lists on the World Wide Web (listed in chapter ten).

Vendors, distributors and wholesalers can become valuable friends and the lifeblood of a business selling to the public. Answer correspondence promptly and pay your bills on time. Establish good credit and as your business expands, your dealings with vendors will too. After all, your business cannot exist without them.

Managing Your Cash Flow

Managing cash flow is a critical element in managing your business. Choose your bank carefully. Look for a neighborhood bank close to your home and one that offers help and advice to small business owners. Remember the banker I mentioned in the last chapter who advocated for me to acquire merchant credit card status? She has also guided me in making other financial decisions regarding my business.

Your Bank Accounts

The IRS will discourage and may even disallow the legitimate business expenses of self-employed people who write both personal and business checks using only one bank account. Don't put off opening a second checking account for your business. If the time comes when your business needs an infusion of cash from your personal account, establish what the IRS calls a paper trail by transferring funds properly. Write a check on your personal account and deposit it into your business account. Call this a "transfer of funds" in your bookkeeping ledger. When your business can pay your personal account back, reverse the process: Write a check from your business account and deposit it into your personal account to pay back your "loan." Not only will the IRS approve, your tax expert will appreciate your effort to make your transactions clear.

Sources of Operating Funds

Scrutinize your present financial situation if you need start-up funds. Do you have enough cash from your savings to have "staying power" until your business can begin to pay you a draw? If not, consider the following ways to raise money without borrowing. You can:

- Cash in savings bonds
- Cash certificates of deposit
- Sell assets such as real estate, cars and other tangible assets

We all experience occasions when we simply must borrow money for our business. If your personal budget cannot come to the rescue, consider the following ways to find money when you need it:

- Borrow on your credit cards, but consider the high interest rates. If you feel positive that such a short-term loan will pay for itself quickly, try this method.
- For large amounts, take out a second home mortgage, also known as a home equity loan. This enables you to use part of your home's equity to fund your business. Bear in mind that if you do this, repaying the loan becomes a business deduction.

Take care not to overdo this to the point where you jeopardize the security of owning your own home.

• You can also make a short-term bank loan using your CD's, "T" bills, or savings accounts as collateral.

• Friends and relatives are also informal sources for borrowing. Don't ask for a "favor." Instead, ask if they wish to invest in you and your idea and give a specific offer of the return they will receive for their loan, not gift. Discuss the offer of paying back the loan with interest. When you agree, draw up an informal written contract.

• Consider a friend or family member who will co-sign a loan with you. This is easier than getting someone to lend you actual cash. Your repayments are a legal business deduction.

Credit Cards

Buying by credit card usually helps your business, but watch commingling again! If you plan to pay for business purchases with a credit card, obtain a new one. Separate your personal purchases from business purchases. Your second card need not be made out to the actual name of your business; your own name will suffice. Make sure you make all payments for business credit card purchases from your business account.

How to Grow Your Business: Writing a Business Plan

I've heard the saying, "If timing is everything, planning is everything else." Many new business owners become intimidated when they first learn they should have a business plan. Think of it as a collection of notes, plans and ideas to guide you into helping your business grow in the most profitable direction.

If you apply for a business loan, however small, your banker will request a business plan, but this is not the only reason you should have one. Financial advisors and your tax preparer may want to see it too. However, you are the most important person that will read your plan.

Preparing the information and organizing and researching it provides you with practical direction about marketing, advertising and bookkeeping. Theoretically, your plan will guide you as you make decisions, set policies and make contingency plans. Think of it as a road map that will help you find your way through unfamiliar territory step by step.

Put It in Writing

Students in my college classes often assure me that they have filed their business plan "in their head." Sorry, but no *written* business plan means you have no plan. It shows you have not yet given your business top priority. My response to those wanting to start a business with no plan is to ask, "Without a plan, how will you measure success and recognize when you've met your goals?"

Business plans need not take weeks to prepare. Use common, everyday language. Remember that class you took in eighth grade about making an outline to organize information? Those roman numerals and capital letters form an easy, sensible way to line up your information. I have prepared dozens of business plans for those who do not type or do not have access to a computer. Copy my list of headings below and fill in the blanks. Complete each heading as thoroughly as possible. Do not assume every reader will know all the details of your business. *Tell* them concisely and precisely in your plan.

A Business Plan Outline

I. TABLE OF CONTENTS

When you have completed your plan, create a table of contents that lists in sequence all of the categories of information and their page numbers. (Make sure you have numbered each page of your plan.)

II. OWNER INFORMATION

Include your name, business name, address and all pertinent phone and fax numbers, websites and e-mail addresses.

III. TYPE OF BUSINESS

Describe the business in detail. "Quilting" is not enough. Do you teach, design, write, quilt for others or perform other services? Name them all.

IV. LEGAL STRUCTURE

State whether your business is a partnership, corporation or proprietorship. Include copies of pertinent legal documents.

V. BUSINESS OBJECTIVE

In a few paragraphs, explain what you want to accomplish through your business. Profit making is too general. Be specific. Profiles of the part-time professionals in this book do not include their business plan. However, if you read carefully, you will find that each person had a goal to achieve. Name yours.

VI. INDUSTRY DATA

Include statistics and other relevant information about the quilting, sewing and crafting business in general. You will find such information in quilt magazines and craft trade journals. Pretend that you must justify to someone else why you have chosen the quilting business. Support your choice by including copies of articles, reports and surveys.

VII. MARKETING PLAN (REVIEW CHAPTER THREE FOR DETAILS)

A. *Customer Profile*
B. *Potential Target Markets*
C. *Marketing Strategies*
D. *Competition*

VIII. IMPLEMENTATION START-UP TIMETABLE

Create a time line of dates proposing when each task will be completed.

IX. BUDGET PROPOSAL, FUNDS REQUIRED AND THEIR USES

List exactly how much money you need to begin and how it will be used.

X. MONTHLY EXPENSES

Make out a budget listing all expected expenses.

XI. CASH FLOW STATEMENT

Show how much you expect to earn and how you will apply earnings to your business expenses.

XII. CASH FLOW STATEMENT FROM LAST YEAR IF YOU ARE ALREADY IN BUSINESS

XIII. PROPRIETARY RIGHTS

A. *Copyrights*
List copyrights you own plus any copyright license you have granted to others. (More about this in chapter six.)
B. *Trademarks*
Include a copy of your trademark registration if applicable.

Think of your business plan as a living document. Consult it regularly. Compare your stated goals with what actually happened. Adjust your plan as you, your business and the external marketplace change. A good plan always keeps owners in touch with the heart of their business.

A Computer for Your Quilt Studio?

Do you wonder if you should computerize your quilt business? A computer may help in your quilting business when:

- You can no longer do everything yourself
- Paperwork cuts into your quilting time
- You need desktop capabilities for a more professional look to your documents
- You need to organize information
- You want to benefit from quilting and other design software
- Bookkeeping chores overwhelm you

Word Processing Software

Computers don't eliminate paper from a business, but they do lessen paperwork, which will provide you with more quilting time. Word processing programs simplify correspondence and instructional writing. You can save your lesson plans, making it easier to revise them.

Data Management Software

Data management simply means organizing information for your quilting business. With appropriate software, you can also manage mailing lists of your customers, vendors and quilt guilds as well as listing the company names and addresses of those who provide you with raw materials. There are several versions of card files used to maintain the names of business contacts. Computerized card files help you organize names and addresses and provide extra space for comments and notes.

Spreadsheet and Bookkeeping Software

Bookkeepers relish bookkeeping chores but quilters often do not. Spreadsheet programs will allow you to record financial income and expenses and help you prepare your income tax returns. Use them to record income and expenses. Accounting programs make it easy to make invoices, bill clients and keep track of what they owe. Other programs allow you to make charts and graphs providing an instant pictorial view of earnings and expenses. Consider QuickBooks made by Intuit, which also produces Quicken. Though both are excellent software programs, the former is a complete accounting program enabling you to use double entry methods where each transaction is entered twice in the ledger—once to record an expenditure and once more to provide details of the expense. Single entry programs such as Quicken, provide only a computerized check register, which lists deposits and expenses without explanation. Business people usually outgrow Quicken while QuickBooks will handle even very large businesses.

Design Software

Computer software allows you to become your own graphic designer. You can customize documents such as brochures, business cards, flyers, letterhead stationery, resumes and even your own newsletter. This software can help teachers create professional-looking handouts and instructions.

Quilters who have graphic capabilities have several specialized quilting programs from which to choose. Today's software will help you design your quilts from start to finish. You can design your own blocks and quilts, and test dozens of color arrangements. Drawing and printing accurate templates is magical. Read Judy Heim's wonderful book, *The Needlecrafter's Computer Companion*, for explicit, easy-to-understand suggestions, reviews and comparisons of computer software for those doing creative work.

You may find it interesting to note that all of the part-time quilting professionals listed in this book use a computer one way or the other. Consider also the benefits of joining other quilters in cyberspace. Contacts, networking, product information, question-and-answer news groups and more await.

As a full-time designer and writer, I have found my computer system has doubled my work output and tripled my income. Though it takes time to learn, the benefits pay off. (See chapter ten for lists of software and World Wide Web sites.)

CHAPTER 5 CHECKLIST

✓ To make a successful transition from hobby to enterprise, you must learn what it takes to treat quilting like a business.

✓ Do your homework and learn about the city, county and state regulations in your geographical area. Following them carefully will help provide credibility to your new business.

✓ Learn how to buy at wholesale prices and to sell at retail. The 50 percent price differential forms the backbone for profit making in the industry.

✓ Apply for and properly use your seller's permit. It offers more benefits than merely enabling you to buy wholesale.

✓ Collect sales taxes and file your forms with your state agency. Take time for fastidious record keeping and budget ahead for paying the sales taxes you collect.

✓ Once your quilting activity becomes a business, look to the IRS for guidance. Request their free literature and follow their statutes to run your business properly and legally.

✓ Learn the details about taking the home office deduction. Once you understand its limitations and benefits, you will find you have nothing to fear if you must face an IRS audit. Deducting a portion of your living expenses and utilities means money in your pocket.

✓ Bookkeeping is essential to all businesses, large or small. Take time to establish an efficient system and maintain it regularly for maximum success and a minimum of headaches. Good records of your deductible expenses prove to the IRS that you are trying to make a profit.

✓ Banking requirements for your business differ slightly from your personal account. Take care to avoid commingling of funds. Both your tax preparer and the IRS will thank you.

✓ Business plans keep you pointed toward success. Don't skip this important step. It's not as complicated as you may think.

✓ Computers can help save time and labor. Has the time come for you to computerize?

BASIC WORLD WIDE WEB AND INTERNET DEFINITIONS

Readers who may be new or unfamiliar with the jargon of the Internet, may find it helpful to review the following definitions and terms before reading the interesting profile of Ozz and Mary Graham.

• *Internet:* An enormous system of computer networks electronically connected to promote an exchange of global information through technology. There is no president, chief operating officer or board of directors. It is self-governed.

• *World Wide Web:* A worldwide electronic medium of communication on the Internet. With appropriate software and a hookup to a service provider, individual computer users throughout the world can be linked to what is popularly called "the Web."

• *Website:* A specific place on the Web where an individual or group can promote their business products, services and other interests. Using a special language called Hyper-Link, a business can create one or more pages of information, enabling users to click on any topic of interest they choose on a specific site. Some websites even provide users with addresses of other sites that offer related information. Individual websites have their own addresses on the Web where users can find them. People access a particular site of desired information by typing in the particular website address.

• *E-mail (Electronic Mail):* A method of instant communication to send and receive messages from one computer to another via the Internet. Once connected to a server (a service that transmits messages for its clients), users can reach any other connected e-mail addressees no matter where in the world they are located.

• *Mailing Lists:* Worldwide groups of people who regularly communicate with each other about a specific, common interest. Members sign up by providing their e-mail address to a mail-service provider, which in turn posts correspondence sent to and received by all members. This way, rather than settling for the opinion of only one person, an individual can request the opinions of the entire group.

• *Chat Groups:* These enable online computer users to communicate directly with each other via their keyboard. This "conversation" may include two or more people actually "chatting" with others simultaneously.

References:

Krol, Ed. *The Whole Internet User's Guide.*
    Sebastopol, CA; O'Reilly & Associates, 1994.
"E-Mail Face-Off." In *Internet World* magazine. Dec. 1996.
    Mecklermedia Corp., 20 Ketchum St., Westport, CT, 06880.

Mary and Ozz Graham—Quilters in Cyberspace

Mary and Osborne (Ozz) Graham have established a strong presence in cyberspace by combining their computing and quilting interests on both the World Wide Web and the Internet. First, Mary and Ozz designed their own website to showcase their products and services. Later, the Grahams established two successful online mailing lists where professional crafters and quilters share advice and resources with one another.

Mary Graham began quilting in 1980 after taking her first quilting class. At the time, Mary, a dedicated cross-stitch enthusiast, had seen three of her original designs published. Says Mary, "Once I started quilting, I could not stop."

Her enthusiasm inspired her to start a local quilt guild in California where she lived at the time. Developing quilting skills was the focus of each meeting. After gaining experience, Mary began teaching classes and workshops for her own guild and for other guilds nearby.

Next, Mary developed her own line of quilt patterns for sale. Shortly after relocating in New Mexico in January 1994, her quilting business took a decidedly different turn. Mary and Ozz entered the world of the Internet.

Though her quilt pattern business had grown successfully, Mary decided to give up marketing the business traditionally. "My whole world changed after cruising the Internet for just a short time," says Mary. "I recognized the marketing potential for my business right from the comfort of my own home using my computer."

Mary quickly joined all the quilt-related chat groups and mailing lists she could find. Reality set in, however, when she learned such groups discouraged discussion of business-related topics even if they concerned quilts.

Ozz had always helped out in the pattern business by filling orders and helping with the bookkeeping, but the Internet intrigued him too, motivating him to contribute more to Mary's business. "Why not start a special forum where members would be encouraged, not prevented from, supporting each other's quilting business interests?" thought both Grahams. "Though we had no idea of how to go about such a venture, we forged ahead anyway," says Mary. "Little did we know how much our world would change."

Quilters from all over the country agreed with the Grahams when they proposed the idea on several quilt hobbyist chat groups. In less than a year, over five hundred professional quilters joined their mailing list, QuiltBiz. Quilters interested in profiting from their skill also wanted a forum on the Internet where they could exchange business-related ideas more freely than chat groups would permit. QuiltBiz came into being to meet this need. I "met" Mary and Ozz Graham and many of the other professional quilters profiled in this book on QuiltBiz.

The success of QuiltBiz led the Grahams to create a QuiltBiz website where members could display their work and market their products. Mary continues, "I had already learned a bit about HTML (hypertext markup language) in creating my own website for my pattern business. I felt professional quilt businesses everywhere could gather in a single place on the Internet to market their products and services rather than struggling for recognition with individual websites.

"The QuiltBiz website developed much faster than I ever imagined," admits Mary. "From marketing my patterns on the Internet, we now host three active mailing-lists and a website." Recently, the Grahams sponsored an online business seminar to help those just starting their businesses or those wanting to expand an established business. Each day, members read information about business topics such as writing a business plan or marketing plan, and pricing ideas. After reading and even downloading the information to their own computers, QuiltBiz members could question and add suggestions, which were answered the next day.

"Next, we added a new mailing list we called NeedleWorks for professional needlework designers. This, of course, led to a new NeedleWorks website showcasing needlework of all types," says Mary. Recently, the Grahams started their third mailing list, Design-Craft, for designers in any craft field. "I never imagined that starting our first mailing list would develop to what we have now. The activity on the QuiltBiz website grows every day. Currently, cyberspace travelers access our site an average of 1,500 times a day."

Ozz still fills orders, manages all the technical work for the lists and websites, and responds to most incoming e-mail questions. Since he still works full time outside of the home, he doesn't have time to do all of the things both Grahams envision.

"After creating all the graphics for our websites, I discovered that other quilt-related websites could use our services too," Mary adds. "Today we create web pages for others who want to see their business on the Internet. QuiltBiz now has a free clip art library for associate members (those who contribute information and tips to QuiltBiz) so they can add them to their own websites."

Mary acknowledges that starting out by sharing with others at no cost to them ended up contributing to the Graham's success because members' referrals and endorsements gave them wide name recognition. The Grahams developed QuiltBiz and their website before charging for ads on it. Explains Mary, "I firmly believe that before you start charging for anything, you should have something established that's worth paying for."

Next, the Grahams undertook another novel approach that garnered the attention of thousands of quilters. They announced an online quilting contest, "The QuiltBiz Cyber-Fiber Challenge," which offered prizes for winning submissions made by participating quilt businesses. Photos of the winning quilts were displayed on the QuiltBiz website.

Today QuiltBiz's members range from one-person, home-based businesses to large, very well-known publishing companies and manufacturers. Shop owners, well-known teachers and lecturers, writers and quilt artists exchange information each day, often answering questions and solving problems for its members.

"Conversation on our mailing list remains informative and open," says Mary. "Larger businesses do not hesitate to offer helpful advice to those just starting. The free exchange of ideas and suggestions that we see everyday inspires us all. Our members have made QuiltBiz the success it is today. We are amazed at the growth we have experienced in only one short year."

Of their future goals: "We plan to have a QuiltBiz co-op bulletin board on the Internet for busi-nesses that want to share booth space expenses at trade shows. We hope to develop a database in which to archive information from the list including contact names and product information."

The Grahams also plan to add a show listing to their website where members can market their products in advance. "We'd also like to grow and expand our websites and hold seminars and discussion groups for members as well as opportunities to meet face-to-face—a sort of QuiltBiz convention," says Mary.

"We plan to make QuiltBiz the central place on the Internet for quilt-related businesses. As for my pattern business that started all of this, it is still doing well on the Internet. Though I don't have as much time to design as I would like to, I still make time for my first love—quilting."

MARY AND OZZ GRAHAM: ON-LINE PRODUCTIONS

℅ QuiltBiz, P.O. Box 30184, Albuquerque, NM 87190-0184

E-mail:

Ozz Graham: ozzg@nmia.com, *Mary Graham:* mgdesign@nmia.com

Websites:

QuiltBiz: http://www.nmia.com/~ozzg/quiltbiz.htm

NeedleWorks: http://www.nmia.com/~ozzg/needle.htm

SELLING YOUR DESIGNS TO MAGAZINES

Quilters, take note! You have many ways to generate income from quilting besides selling directly to customers. Why not sell an original quilt design to a magazine *before* selling it to a consumer? Here's how the system works:

- Magazines devoted to quilting need fresh, new ideas and designs to publish.
- Readers and hobbyists need inspiration and motivation from quilt designers so they can learn about the latest quilting trends and techniques.
- Manufacturers of quilt supplies need designers/writers to create designs that will motivate consumers to buy their products. Most companies provide complimentary supplies to professional designers, enabling them to learn about and use a steady stream of new products in their work.

Readers benefit when they learn how to use products required in a specific project. Manufacturers recognize the connection between writing designers and consumers, and many offer endorsement fees to designers, who mention products by name in their articles. More about this later in this chapter.

How to Start

Before submitting your quilt designs to any magazine, study at least three issues of the magazine so you can determine if your design is appropriate for the publication. Editors agree that too often, designers submit designs without taking the time to learn about the magazine's style, needs and format.

Help yourself along by reading *Writer's Market*, published annually by Writer's Digest Books. This hefty book describes both the needs and readership of most American magazines. You will also find a complete list of quilting magazines in chapter ten.

After studying several quilt and craft publications, select those you find appropriate for your work. Take time to match carefully. Send traditional designs to publications that specialize in designs that have borne the test of time such as *Traditional Quilter* or *Quilter's Newsletter*. But send contemporary ideas to *Art Quilts* or others that feature modern quilt designs.

Magazines such as *Threads*, prefer narrative articles about how a designer works over step-by-step how-to's, which include actual instructions to complete a project. Recent issues featured quilters sharing their techniques for dyeing fabric, binding quilts and the art of appliqué, to name a few. *Piecework Magazine* prefers to focus on the historical aspects of the quilts they feature. *Professional Quilter* magazine seeks articles about the profitable side of quilting. *Crafts* magazine prefers simple, theme and holiday quilts. They often buy quilt designs that incorporate another type of craft into the quilt, such as painting, stenciling or photo-imaging.

Selling your designs depends on your ability to choose the proper publication to offer your design idea to. Do not limit yourself to submitting quilt designs exclusively. Readers want topically related ideas too. Recently, I have written articles about:

- How to choose, collect and store fabrics and notions for nostalgic quilts
- How to organize a sewing studio
- Color and design basics
- How to hand-paint fabrics
- Stained glass quilting techniques
- How to structure a series of quilting classes
- Trapunto for beginners
- How to use marbleized fabrics

Assess the tips and skills you have to share that will bring you extra profit. Once you have selected a few appropriate publications, write to each one. Request a set of writer's guidelines. Publishers provide these at no cost if you enclose a self-addressed, stamped envelope with your request. Study the guidelines carefully. Editors and publishers describe exactly what they want, what they need and how they want designs presented to them. Will they accept your text on paper or require a computer disk? Do they limit article length? Do they pay extra for photos? Will they ask you to send them your quilt for photography or accept your snapshots? Note their deadlines for each issue. When do they wish to see holiday items? Do they require fabric swatches? Will they accept computer-generated designs? You will receive answers to these questions in the guidelines from each publication.

What's a Query Letter?

After studying the guidelines, the next step is to submit a query letter describing your idea, design or article to the right magazine. You can offer a completed project or propose to make one for the magazine. Query letters begin a line of communication between the writer/designer and the editor/publisher. Check the books listed in chapter ten about how to write top-notch queries.

Approach the editor in a businesslike way. Propose your idea clearly and assertively. The style, grammar and word usage in your query letter serve as an example to the editor about how you will prepare your articles and instructions. Thus, make your query letter your best effort by using professional letter-writing techniques. Tell the editor about you and your qualifications by including a brochure, business card or resume. If you are proposing a quilt design, include a photo or two. All of these enhance your chances of acceptance.

Working With Editors and Publishers

Editors who find your quilt article or design of interest will either call or write to you. Usually they propose an amount they will pay to buy your design article. Occasionally they will ask you, the designer, how much you want for the article. Novice writers may feel unprepared when this occurs, having no idea of the going rates.

Save yourself some anxiety and research this issue beforehand. Contact other quilt designers and ask. Join the Society of Craft Designers. Tips in their excellent newsletter can help prepare you with the buying and selling procedures of designs. The newsletter also offers regular tips about pricing so you will neither price yourself out of the market nor sell yourself too cheaply.

After you agree on a price, follow the editors' instructions. They will tell you when and how to send your item plus how they want the instructional text. They may make suggestions or changes or accept your entire idea. Remember, when the magazine's photographers finish working with your quilt, they usually return it to you unless you have made other arrangements.

Publishers and editors will send you a contract telling you what rights they wish to buy to publish your design. Read a contract carefully as it tells you:

1. The deadline when you must submit your work.

2. When they will pay you—on acceptance or publication. "Acceptance" means you receive payment when the design is accepted even though it may not be published for many months. "Publication" means you will not receive payment until the design appears in print, a practice that delays payment.

3. Which issue of the magazine will contain your design.

4. How many complimentary issues containing your design they will send to you upon publication. Save tear sheets from magazines that have published your work to put in your portfolio. Use them in the future when you contact manufacturers to request complimentary products. Tear sheets lend credibility to your status as a designer. Manufacturers who provide complimentary products *request* tear sheets or a photocopy of your article before paying you an endorsement fee. Tear sheets prove your endorsement of their product, which in turn triggers payment of the fee.

If a magazine editor sees your photo of a completed quilt design, all you need to do is send the quilt for photography as requested. However, most established quilt designers prefer to make a proposal *before* completing a quilt. Once the editor accepts the idea, the designer makes the quilt on commission following the guidelines suggested by the editor. When you agree to design a quilted project for publication rather than selling a quilt you had previously completed, you must write another letter—to manufacturers.

Business Networks That Help Designers

Membership in craft organizations such as the Society of Craft Designers (SCD) and the Hobby Industry Association (HIA) provides you with help selling your designs. Their annual listings enable you to locate manufacturers of quilt and sewing products that offer complimentary supplies. (See chapter nine for more information about the help that networking organizations such as these can offer.)

Approach manufacturers in the same professional manner you used to contact magazine editors. Prepare to tell them how you will use their product and exactly how much you need. Gather supply catalogs from companies with whom you want to deal. Catalog details will help you make selections. Manufacturers want proof of your professional status to separate you from hobbyists seeking "freebies." They may ask what professional organizations you belong to and check your membership status before agreeing to ship goods to you.

I reassure manufacturers that I will make good use of their products by sending them a copy of the magazine's contract letter commissioning me to design a quilt for them. This establishes beyond a doubt how I will use complimentary products.

Some companies provide products and pay an endorsement fee as well. Others provide only complimentary products and will not pay endorsement fees. Manufacturers with endorsement fee programs pay them directly to you after publication. This money is in addition to the payment you receive from the magazine for writing the design article.

Once on the mailing list of a specific manufacturer, you will receive information about upcoming and new products. Many companies routinely send samples of new products to designers on their list.

Writing Instructions

Accuracy is prime in writing instructions. Details about how to make templates, cut fabric and sew the project must leave no margin for error. Write as if your reader is making her first quilt and leave nothing unsaid.

Take care to list the steps in proper order, first to last. Sequence is vital for readers at all levels. Though most editors have a staff to edit your instructions, do not rely on them to make corrections or calculations for you. If you make it simple for your editor to work from your instructions, they will be more apt to buy your future designs.

When you have all of your raw materials, begin the project, but don't work straight through to completion. If you plan to sell design articles, you must write the instructions as you go.

You will develop your own system or you may follow the procedure I use below for writing clear, complete and accurate instructions:

1. List all of the materials you will use in descending order of importance. Don't worry if you find yourself adding to the list as you go. Each time you pick up a new tool or notion, add it to your supply list.
2. Provide measurements for the overall quilt and for the blocks, sashing, borders and so on.
3. Add cutting instructions.
4. Make an outline of each template you use, if any.
5. When you have completed one unit of the project, stop sewing.
6. Go to your typewriter or computer and write down every step you took. Print out these instructions and consider them your first draft.
7. Resume working, but this time follow your written instructions—not your memory. Have you included every step?

8. Revise and add any missing information. Create a second draft.

9. Working from your instructions *only*, repeat the sewing and writing process until you have completed the project. Print out a third draft.

10. After you have finished writing the instructions, distance yourself from it for a few days.

11. Whenever possible, ask a friend to make a design unit following your written instructions without asking for your help.

12. Keeping in mind any suggestions made by your friend, revise, correct and reword the instructions for the last time. Try to make your instructions stand alone.

Teachers have an additional method to test their instructions. With the agreement of a particular class, known as a "pilot" class, students agree to test the pattern as a group. Their success in producing the project indicates that the instructions have merit. However, if the class experiences frustration following your instructions or if you see that your pattern contains inaccuracies, you know your text requires additional clarification before submitting it to an editor.

Record Keeping

Keep good records about each project. I keep all original hard copies, contracts, instructions, diagrams and so on, in a file folder for each magazine I write for. Note how long it takes you to make the project. Keep track of the time you spend writing, too. With experience, you will learn to set a fair price for your work.

Expect rejections when you begin submitting to magazines. Everyone who submits regularly receives them, so use them to learn. Study, date and file each rejection. Study the rejected projects too. Can you improve the design or the instructions? Rewrite if necessary and promptly resubmit it to another magazine from your list.

Many rejections have to do with timeliness. Perhaps a quilt with a similar theme or color scheme is in the works for an upcoming issue. Perhaps what you proposed appeared in a previous issue. Remember, this is why you should check past copies of the publication. Writer's magazines tell us that if we don't receive rejections regularly, we are not sending proposals to enough publications.

Royalty Publishing

Beginning craft writers may start writing about quilts for magazines, but don't overlook finding a publisher for your books, design pamphlets and patterns in the future. Royalty publishers contract with a writer to publish a book. Such companies invest heavily in a book project, including the editing, printing, advertising, distribution and other costs. Writers receive a royalty or a portion of the proceeds of each copy sold.

Space here does not permit me to focus on writing or publishing in general, but you can learn about the process from these four books:

1. *Writer's Market* by Writer's Digest Books provides information about most publishers, what they want and who to contact.
2. *Insider's Guide to Book Editors, Publishers and Agents* by Jeff Herman, Prima Publishing.
3. *How Write a Book Proposal* by Michael Larsen, Writer's Digest Books.
4. *Write the Perfect Book Proposal* by Jeff Herman and Deborah M. Adams, John Wiley & Sons, Inc.

When you feel ready to write a book, begin looking for a publisher. Quilters may begin with publishers who specialize in the topic, such as Interweave Press, C & T Publishers or That Patchwork Place. You can also choose a mainstream publisher interested in crafts.

Self-Publishing

Advantages and disadvantages come with self-publishing. On one hand, you get to keep the full retail price yourself as opposed to only the percentage you receive from a publisher. However, you must pay all of the expenses of publishing. Royalty publishers advertise your book, get it into bookstores and try to get book clubs to offer it, increasing profits for everyone. Self-publishers face a tough problem finding adequate distribution to shops, a fact that keeps many from trying to publish this way.

Read *The Complete Guide to Self-Publishing* by Tom and Marilyn Ross (Writer's Digest Books) and *Publish It Yourself*, which was self-published by Charles Chickadel. The authors guide you in the steps of preparing and manufacturing your own books, patterns, booklets and so on. Consult the latest *Writer's Market*, which lists companies that print and manufacture books and other printed material.

Here are the steps I followed in self-publishing and selling six instructional design booklets for advanced stitchers.

- I composed the instructional text.
- I hand-drew and colored the graphs and charts, which is now possible to do on computers.
- I took quality snapshots of each project from close-up and afar.

- I purchased report covers with a sliding spine and clear covers.
- Local printers produced the copy.
- My family and I collated the pages and inserted them into the covers.
- We added two colored snapshots to the cover page, beneath the plastic cover.
- I placed classified ads in selected publications.
- Individual buyers bought the booklets via mail order.
- I wrapped, packaged and mailed each order myself.
- Occasionally, I sold several booklets at once to shops around the country.

Demand kept the series in print for nine years. Today, I continue to give workshops teaching the techniques in the booklets and to sell copies during lectures and classes. So can you. (See chapter ten for recommended books to help you polish your writing skills.)

About Copyright

Copyright questions concerning both written work and design projects generate more interest, confusion and misinformation than any other topic among my college students and clients. Sadly, the first thing some ask is how much they can alter the work of another to claim it as their own. Usually, the same individual expresses determination to prevent anyone from altering *their* original designs.

People usually assume that copyright law is incomprehensible and inconsistent. Not so. Let's define copyright in the same words the Copyright Office uses. From the book, *Copyright Law of the United States of America*, Title #17, Section #102: "The heart of the new copyright law is the grant of certain exclusive rights to the copyright owner. The exclusive rights of an author/owner last for fifty years after the owner's death and appear below:

- to reproduce the copyrighted work in copies
- to prepare derivative works
- to distribute to the public
- to perform publicly
- to display publicly certain works

"The new law (after January 1, 1978) provides that anyone who violates any of the exclusive rights of the copyright owner . . . is an infringer of copyright.' The copyright owner may file an infringement action in federal court against the infringer within three years from the date of the infringement."

Copyright and Quilters

How does copyright apply to quilters? Copyright provides writers and designers with the sole right to make copies, reproduce or distribute their work, or prepare derivative works. Others must secure *written* permission before using another's copyrighted work.

Let's take a simple example. Jane Doe designs and makes a sampler quilt. Applying the rules above she may:

- Reproduce her instructions, templates and designs, and distribute them to students who take her workshops. No one else may do this without her *written* permission.
- Copy her own work into a miniature quilt, thus preparing a derivative work.
- Give or sell copies of her instructions to anyone she chooses.
- Present a lecture about her process and show slides of the work.
- Display the quilt at local, regional and national exhibits.

Jane cannot copyright the design while the idea remains in her mind. However, the moment she "fixes the work in a tangible medium" (on paper and/or fabric), she has protection by common copyright law. Jane only needs to place the copyright symbol (©) followed by the year, her name or the name of her business prominently on her work to claim copyright ownership.

Registering her copyright is another matter. Before Jane can take infringement action against Mary, who copied Jane's instructions and distributed them to members of her guild at no charge, Jane must register her copyright with the Library of Congress. (You'll find the address on page 105 of this chapter.)

People often assume you may *give away* the work of another as long as you do not make a profit. Not so. The design belongs to Jane and no one can give it away to others without her permission.

Fair Use of Copyrighted Material

"Fair use" doctrine also generates confusion for many, but the law is clear. Quoting directly from copyright literature, we learn when we can use the copyrighted work of another without permission. " 'Fair use' " allows others to use a small part of your copyrighted work without your permission for: review, comment, scholarship, research, news reporting and teaching."

That last word, "teaching," brings forth the most controversy. Copying the handouts of another and teaching it to a guild violates the owner's copyright. Quilting teachers, at times, interpret the law to say that they may copy another teacher's handouts because the activity remains as teaching.

Copyright law (Section #110) explains that classroom teaching exemption applies to nonprofit educational institutions such as primary schools, high schools, colleges and universities. Guilds, seminars and conventions may have nonprofit status but are not defined as institutions of learning. The copyright handbook makes this distinction clear.

Since teachers may make copies of patterns for educational use in *nonprofit* settings, a quilting instructor may make copies from a current quilt magazine for each student in her high school class. The same teacher may *not* use the *same* reprint to teach in a local quilt shop or seminar. Why not? Because these are for-profit settings, not to be confused with the nonprofit status of the group (Section #107). When groups or individuals photocopy the work of others and distribute them even for nonprofit purposes, they deprive the legal owner from profiting from her design.

Purchasers of commercial patterns expect to recreate designs according to copyrighted instructions. This is "fair use." You can make a baby quilt from a pattern to keep for yourself and one to give as a gift. However, if you try to profit from the design or mass produce the quilt for sale in nearby shops, you would surely hear from the pattern company. They have the right to seek an injunction to stop further production and force you to turn over profits that are legally theirs.

Works in Public Domain

Quilters frequently ask when a work enters public domain, enabling them to use or copy a design freely. Without renewal, "Any copyright existing before January 1, 1978, shall endure for 28 years from the date of registration," states the law.

Questions arise when you try to determine the copyright status of a work *before* the new 1978 law took effect. Works published 28 years ago but less than 75 years ago received protection for 28 years *unless* the owner filed a renewal. Few designers renewed copyrights during this period but if they did, they received an additional 47-year renewal term.

Let's say you found an unusual quilt block and article in a magazine published in 1963. Without renewal, this material became public domain in 1991, when anyone could use it. Contact the Library of Congress to see if the writer filed a renewal. You can do research yourself at certain libraries throughout the U.S., or pay $20 per hour for the Copyright Office to do it for you. Request a free list of research libraries containing copyright, patent and trademark data from the Copyright Office.

If you cannot determine whether or not a renewal exists, subtract seventy-five years from the current year to be absolutely safe. Anything copyrighted before that date is now in public domain.

What about traditional quilt patterns like Log Cabin or Wedding Ring? These designs have been in the public domain for decades and anyone can design a quilt using these patterns. If you design an original quilt based upon Log Cabin, for example, you can copyright the quilt's *design*. Recognize that you are not copyrighting Log Cabin, but how you incorporated a traditional pattern like this into your quilt. Your design copyright covers how you used color, fabric, scale, overall measurements and borders. Copyright protection also extends to your instructions and template drawings for the quilt.

Exclusivity is not necessary with copyrights as it is with patents and trademarks. Thus, an East Coast quilter may design her interpretation of the ocean shore on a quilt while a West Coast artist designs one nearly identical. Both may receive a copyright.

Get in the habit of documenting your quilt designs. Take a series of photos to show the evolution of the quilt in progress. I usually start by photographing all of the materials I will be using by placing them in a pile on the floor or table. Later, I show the cutting process followed by basting, piecing, hand-quilting and then finishing the quilt. Placing the dates on the photos thus documents that the project originated with me.

Some people believe a copyrighted design becomes theirs if they make a certain percentage of changes. Again, not so. Copyright law states that modifying someone else's design is "preparing a derivative work." Changing the size of a quilt or altering the original colors, fabric and other details does not create an original work.

If you alter an existing design, remember, the crafting/quilting world is small and mass communication is vast. If a copyright holder of an original design learns of your copy and starts legal action, prepare to defend the similarities in court. If a court determines that your altered design used a "substantial part of a copyrighted design," you may find yourself in violation of copyright laws no matter how many changes you made. Fines range up to $25,000 and can include legal fees.

First Rights, All Rights, Reprint Rights

Publishers and editors buy the rights to a work from a writer or designer in varying forms and degrees. The originator of a work owns all rights to it until he or she decides to sell all or a portion of these rights to another for publication or other public use.

Quilt designers and writers must understand the types of rights so they can:

1. Make sure they receive adequate compensation for their work.
2. Understand how much of the rights to the original work (if any) returns to them after publication for future additional use.

The handbook from the Library of Congress, *Copyright Law of the U.S.* (Circular #92), provides the definitive source of copyright information. The book lists the following types of rights:

1. *First serial rights* means you offer the right to publish your article or design for the first time in any periodical. Afterward, the rights to the material revert to the writer. When material is excerpted from an upcoming book and appears in a magazine or newspaper prior to book publication, this also constitutes first serial rights.

2. *One-time rights* differs from first serial rights in that the magazine has no guarantee that they will be the first to publish the work.

3. *Second serial (reprint) rights* gives a magazine the opportunity to print an article or design after it has appeared in another publication. The term also refers to selling a part of a book to a newspaper or magazine after the book has been published.

4. *All rights.* Some magazines buy all rights, especially of designs. Designers who sell this way may not use the material in its present form elsewhere. If you think you may want to use the material later (perhaps in book form), avoid selling all rights. Some editors will reassign rights to a designer after a given period, such as one year.

5. *Simultaneous rights* covers articles and designs sold to noncompeting publications. You may sell, for example, a Christmas quilt to a quilting magazine and to a religious magazine featuring holiday crafts. Remember to advise an editor when your design is a simultaneous submission to another market.

6. *First serial rights* are sold to a specific publication, assuring them that they will be the first to publish the material although it may be subsequently published again by another publisher.

7. *Foreign serial rights.* You may resell a design published in the U.S. to an international magazine if you sold only first U.S. serial rights to an American publisher.

8. *Subsidiary rights* appear in a book contract. These may include various rights for audio tapes or videotapes, for example.

Registering Your Work

Registering for copyright costs $20 per filing. Before you conclude that it will cost a fortune to register several quilts, consider the Form GR/CP. It allows you to cover several works in a series under one copyright.

If you decide to apply for copyright protection, the Copyright Office will send forms at no cost. They also send instructions on how to fill out the forms. Quilter's needs would be covered with one or more of the following forms:

• *Form TX* covers literary works. This includes patterns, instructions, template drawings, articles and books.

• *Form VA* (Visual Arts) protects creations such as statues, wall hangings, framed pictures and so on. The copyright office requires photos of your designs.

• *Form GR* (Group Registration) covers the copyrighting of a line of similar items. A series of wall hangings for holidays or a line of paper-piecing patterns are examples. Form GR permits you to register similar works with one copyright for a single fee.

The Library of Congress is one of America's user-friendly bureaucracies. They go to great lengths to help with copyright questions and problems. They offer a large list of free publications. Write and request the following *free* circulars from the Library of Congress, U.S. Copyright Office, Washington, DC 20559:

Circular 1 Copyright Basics

Circular 2 Free Publications on Copyright

Circular 3 Copyright Notice

Circular 4 Copyright Fees

Circular R1c Copyright Registration Procedures

Circular R15 Renewal of Copyright

Circular 15a Duration of Copyright

Circular R99 Highlights of the New Copyright Law

Circular R21 Reproduction of Copyrighted Works by Educators and Librarians

Circular 40 Copy Registration for Works of the Visual Arts

Circular 40a Deposit Requirements for Registration of Claims to Copyright in Visual
   Arts Material

Circular 96 Material Not Subject to Copyright

CHAPTER 6 CHECKLIST

✓ Selling a quilt itself is not the only way to profit from your quilting skills. Writing about quilts and selling original designs offer many profitable opportunities for quilters who want to make extra money.

✓ Before offering your designs to a magazine, you *must* study past issues. Review the list of quilting magazines in chapter ten for titles and names of magazine editors.

✓ Preparing accurate instructions is the most important aspect of writing for the quilt market. Computer users will find their computer invaluable for writing, editing and revising instructions as they actually make the quilt project.

✓ When you have gathered sufficient experience writing articles about quilting, consider writing a book. Though this is a serious commitment of time and energy, it is both satisfying and creative, and adds highly to your professional credibility.

✓ Learn the differences between royalty publishing and self-publishing. Many new quilt designers can break into writing by self-publishing patterns and instructional design leaflets.

✓ Complimentary supplies from manufacturers offer many benefits, as do endorsement fees. Search out companies who offer both and treasure your relationship with them. Cooperating with such companies can greatly expand your quilting income.

✓ Study copyright law to minimize confusion and inaccurate advice from others. The Library of Congress offers much gracious and generous support and information. Never take the design of another and alter it to call it your own original. This is unethical, illegal and unsatisfying from the creative, artistic point of view.

✓ Make sure you understand that copyright "fair use" for teaching purposes excludes you from using copyrighted material when teaching for guilds and seminars. Educational settings permit such use. These are defined as kindergarten through college-level classes, not quilt shop or guild classes.

MORNA MCEVER
GOLLETZ—
PUBLISHER AND
EDITOR OF *THE
PROFESSIONAL
QUILTER* AND
PROFESSIONAL
QUILTMAKER

PHOTO COURTESY OF THE SENTINEL, CARLISLE, PA

Morna McEver Golletz wears two hats of great interest to readers of this book. She makes contemporary quilts and accessories for sale, and publishes *The Professional Quilter*, a quarterly publication for quilters seeking to profit from their skills.

Allow me to first introduce you to Morna, the successful quiltmaker whose passion for sewing began at the tender age of three. She was in charge of threading needles for her great-great-grandmother, who could no longer see well enough to

thread them herself. Morna next began sewing doll clothes for her dolls, which led to her first "business" at the age of about ten—selling doll outfits to her friends.

Quilting has been a part of Morna's life since 1977 when she approached a woman who was demonstrating at a craft show and asked about lessons. "After the first class, I bought a book of block patterns, went through my sewing scraps and proceeded to make umpteen pillows. I knew I was hooked," admits Morna.

After completing several full-sized quilts, she realized she needed to support her quilting habit to continue buying fabric. She called the local school and asked if she could teach quilting for its adult education program. "It was the perfect way to pay for fabrics and supplies," says Morna.

When Morna and her husband relocated from Connecticut to Pennsylvania, she decided to focus on teaching quilting as a freelancer. Setting up a studio in her home, she advertised for students in the local paper and the Newcomer's Club. Soon afterward, she began teaching at a local store and in the adult education system.

Seeking to expand, Morna says, "I had many quilts and quilted items and since I loved going to craft shows, why not sell my work at craft shows?" She began doing holiday home shows and then joined a small crafts cooperative at the local YMCA. From there she applied for juried membership in the Creative

Hand, a highly professional crafts cooperative.

"I was the co-op's only quilter," says Morna, who sold contemporary wall hangings as well as smaller accessory items. "It was a great learning experience. We operated a full-time store in a mall, so I picked up a lot of valuable business skills."

Her association with the cooperative led to individual commission work, something Morna found creatively rewarding. A second family move required Morna to commute seventy miles to the co-op. "While my co-op membership was rewarding financially and emotionally, I had to evaluate my family priorities and leave the co-op," she explains.

Over the next six years, Morna focused on teaching quilting, selling commission pieces and writing. During this period, she enrolled in graduate school at Temple University receiving her master's degree in journalism in 1992. Unknowingly at the time, her decision became the perfect segue taking her from quilter to publisher.

And now, let's meet Morna—writer, editor and publisher. "To expand my career as a quilter, I subscribed to *The Professional Quilter*. After selling a quilt-maker's profile to *Quilter's*

Newsletter Magazine, I was talking to one of the editors only to realize she was the original publisher of *The Professional Quilter* and had begun the process of selling it." (Jeannie Spears, its founder, had moved to Colorado to join the staff at *Quilter's Newsletter*.)

Morna purchased the magazine in April 1994 after it had ceased publication six months earlier. "When I first purchased the magazine, I received a database of previous customers and the trade name. Marketing was a challenge because though the magazine had name recognition, it had ceased publication."

Morna used direct mail to contact six thousand former subscribers from around the world to get the magazine up and running again. "I advertised in consumer quilt magazines, tracking my database to learn which ads generated the best response. Today I attend both national retail and wholesale quilt shows. The Quilt Market/Festival in Houston is important to me as it draws such large crowds of my niche market. I also attend larger regional quilt shows such as the Quilters Heritage Celebration in Lancaster, Pennsylvania, and the Pennsylvania Quilt Extravaganza outside Philadelphia.

"Quilt shows benefit me not only because I sell a product, but because I can interact with my customers. I find I need both wholesale and retail shows because, though I have a tightly niched market, there is a definite crossover, for example, pattern designers and shop owners at wholesale shows, teachers and commission quilters at retail shows. The majority of my sales at trade shows are retail sales."

"I also send flyers to larger quilt shows I cannot attend personally. Members of my guild take 500-1,000 flyers to leave on information tables. Some guilds write requesting a door prize. If I donate, I send flyers to distribute in exchange."

Today, as publisher, Morna fills her day with a variety of activities including editing, advertising, handling circulation and maintaining her marketing plan. "My biggest challenge has been learning the business aspects of the magazine," says Morna. "I think this is true for many people in the creative world. It's much more fun to just quilt.

"I find it very rewarding to combine publishing and writing with quilting," says Morna. "I feel I am making a contribution, helping others who want to earn money through quilting."

If you think writing for *The Professional Quilter* appeals to you, write to Morna and request a set of her writers' guidelines plus a list of topics she would like to include in upcoming issues of the magazine.

MORNA McEVER GOLLETZ: PROFESSIONAL QUILTER MAGAZINE

104 Bramblewood Lane, Lewisberry, PA 17339-9535

Phone:

(717) 691-8176

Fax:

(717) 691-8176

E-mail:

ProQuilters@aol.com

HAVE YOU CONSIDERED TEACHING?

Ah, teaching. A wonderful way to affirm your own skills while sharing them with others. Teaching is a serious business and can stand alone as a full-time moneymaker. Read Karen Comb's (page 125) and Daphne Greig's (page 50) profiles for inspiration about this profitable quilting activity.

Teachers help to maintain the historical and technical aspects of quilting along with teaching basic skills. The more techniques students know and understand, the more enthusiastic they become. Enthusiastic quilters make satisfied customers, which keeps the industry growing. Witness the sales figures for fabric and quilt-related materials in chapter one. Eager, satisfied customers continue to take classes. Thus, the quilting world comes full circle.

Your Own Teaching Studio

Operating a teaching studio from home can be convenient, satisfying and profitable. You can:

- Work without a supervisor
- Set your own policies
- Bypass federal, state or local regulations
- Maintain very low overhead costs
- Choose your pace by teaching on weekdays, evenings or weekends
- Take full responsibility to make your teaching business grow

Do not assume that home teaching offers only benefits. Take time to consider challenging issues as well:

- You will have no guaranteed income. You alone determine your profit and expenses.
- You must pay federal and state income and sales taxes yourself. You must set aside part of your earnings for this for you can no longer count on automatic withholding from an employer.
- You must maintain a fastidious bookkeeping system or hire someone else to do it for you. Remember, as mentioned in chapter five, the IRS *requires* you to show a profit motive.
- Teaching where you live requires organization. Confusion of roles may occur as you learn to distinguish working from home from relaxing there. This troubles some who consider "home" as a refuge—a place only to "live." Now, a part of your home will become your classroom as well.
- Good housekeeping is required. You must maintain a comfortable, organized teaching studio and a presentable bathroom nearby for students.

Preparing to Teach

If you are seriously considering teaching from home, recognize that you must develop expertise in your subject before you can teach it to someone else. Enthusiasm and love of quilting will not substitute for knowledge and thorough preparation. Teaching as a business requires that you also learn how to:

1. Prepare thoroughly—the most important element!
2. Organize your time schedule, studio, paperwork and class content
3. Select sound teaching methods
4. Create an interesting program of classes
5. Prepare interesting, challenging lesson plans
6. Set clear goals for each class and each learning level
7. Offer irresistible projects and quality supplies
8. Advertise and market your classes
9. Set your fees
10. Select and buy supplies
11. Find other ways to profit when classes are not in session or business is slow
12. Keep separate records to track profitability of your classes
13. Prepare effective evaluation sheets for students to fill out after each class. These sheets provide continual marketing information about your classes

Where Will You Teach?

Start your teaching studio by identifying the area you will use as a classroom. If you plan to take the home office deduction described in chapter five, you must consider exclusive use and other limitations.

If you do not plan to take this deduction, your choices become easier. All you need is a clean, well-lighted room with table(s) and chairs for students and a bathroom nearby. Consider converting a large, unused bedroom, family room or garage if you want a permanent arrangement. However, if you have space limitations, you can also clear off your dining room table each time you have a class.

Students need quiet class time to learn. Remember, they pay for your exclusive time during class sessions. Place your pets outside. Housemates must understand that the classroom area is off limits while students are present. Small children may require care and supervision by someone else while you have a class in session, or limit yourself to teach only during nap times or school hours. I even turn off the ringers on my personal and business phones, letting the answering machines take over. This eliminates maddening, ringing telephones during class time.

Finding Students

Before finding students to fill your classes, you must do your marketing. Draw up a profile of your typical student. Below are questions for which you must provide answers:

1. Who are your most likely potential students?
2. Are they retired people or working parents?
3. Does age play a role?
4. Will they be able to find your studio easily?
5. Do they live nearby? Is transportation available for those who live farther away?
6. How do you plan to let them know about your classes and services?
7. What do they want to learn? Basic techniques? Varied projects? Theory?
8. Will most students come to you at a beginning, intermediate or advanced level?
9. Can everyone who wants to take your classes afford them?
10. Do you plan to order supplies and resell them to your students?
11. Will students buy supplies from a nearby shop? Teaching from home can create problems with local quilt shop owners. I suggest you visit nearby shops and tell them of your plans. Many teachers receive a discount for themselves and their students from neighborhood shops. Others bring materials from a shop to sell in

their home studio if the shop owner agrees to this arrangement. Recognize that you may find yourself in direct competition with a nearby shop whose owner may view you as a potential business threat. Strive for a working relationship from the beginning with local shop owners so that everyone benefits.

12. Learn about your competition and make note of their services and schedules.
13. Do other teachers offer what you do?
14. What can you offer that they do not?
15. What do they charge for classes?
16. How do you plan to position yourself in your local market?

If you live in an affluent area, teaching classes on Victorian embellishment and silk ribbon embroidery on quilts may be a great idea. These trends are strong today. However, if you live in or near an economically distressed area, bed quilts, quilted jackets and gifts may appeal to your market more. Learn as much as possible about your market *before* you start.

Setting Fees

Everyone wants a foolproof fee system that guarantees a profit, but no perfect formula exists that will suit everyone, everywhere. Teachers must take several factors into consideration to arrive at their own formulas:

Geographic Location

Economic conditions, preferences and lifestyles vary from large urban areas to small rural communities, and from one U.S. coast to another. You must learn about the external marketplace where you live before you can begin setting realistic prices.

Check Out the Competition

Research what other teachers charge in your community. Don't limit yourself to only checking with quilting teachers. Find out about teachers who conduct classes in music, language, aerobics and other crafts. Check to learn if students pay by the hour, class or an entire series of classes. Start with the yellow pages in your phone directory and make inquiring phone calls. Contact teachers who advertise in the classified section of your local newspaper too. Find out all you can about how they operate.

Record your findings and call your local parks and recreation department next. What types of classes do they offer? How do they charge? Add this to your notes.

Now, call or write the community colleges in your area. Survey their offerings and prices. Last, call quilt shops nearby and up to one hundred miles away. What do they charge? How long do they run each class and what topics do they offer?

Compile the information you've gathered to guide you in creating the perfect price-setting formula for you. Average the prices charged by nearby quilt shops. Compare this to the fees set by adult programs and colleges. Now you know what the market will bear in your particular community.

Next, determine the least amount of money you will accept to set aside a regular time for teaching. Consider canceling any class so small that it fails to generate your stated minimum income per class.

Years ago, when I added home classes to my college classes, I did my own research. Below you will find my resulting formula.

1. Our community college charges an average of $60 for a six-week session of two hours each for several needlework and quilting classes.
2. Our parks and recreation program charges $45 for classes that run for six weeks at two hours each.
3. Two quilt shops nearby charge $65 for an all-day, six-hour class.
4. Piano and art teachers advertising in the newspaper charge $20 per hour for individualized instruction.

Here is the breakdown of what students pay:

Community college:	$5 per hour ($60 divided by twelve hours of instruction)
Parks and recreation:	$3.75 per hour ($45 divided by twelve hours of instruction)
Quilt shops:	$10.80 per hour ($65 divided by six hours of instruction)
Music and art teachers:	$20 per hour

The figures above average $9.89 per hour, which rounds off to $10 per hour. Here's how I applied this figure to set my teaching fee. I charge $30 per person for a five-week session of two hours each. In a class of five students, each class generates a total of $150 or $30 per session, $15 per hour. I take up to ten students at a time—the limit for comfortable seating in my studio. I cancel classes that register three students or less, for this reduces my class income to $90. Divided by five two-hour sessions, this equals only $9 per hour. Writing and designing pay more than this, so it makes more sense to turn to these activities and reschedule when enrollment picks up. Over the years, I've run as many as four regular weekly classes during weekdays, evenings and occasional Saturdays.

Workshop Topics

Day-long workshops work well too. Many special quilting techniques lend themselves to this format. Charge enough to make sure that your profit does not fall below your minimum hourly amount. Below you will find the most popular one-day topics I offer. Expand this list by adding your specialties.

- Basic classes for beginners
- Color and design theory
- Dyeing and hand-painting fabric
- Classes for intermediate and advanced students
- Joining quilt-as-you-go blocks
- Adding borders and binding
- A Cathedral Windows workshop
- Trapunto
- Shadow quilting
- Stained glass quilts
- Wearables
- Combining quilting with knitting and crochet
- Fine appliqué

Advertising Your Classes

You have many options to let others know about your classes. Consider the following:

1. Advertise in the classified section of local newspapers.
2. Advertise in the yellow pages of your local telephone book.
3. Place flyers in local gathering places such as senior centers, recreation centers, shops, adult schools and libraries.
4. Leave brochures, business cards and flyers at your Chamber of Commerce office.
5. Write interesting press releases for your local newspaper mentioning your classes within the text.
6. Distribute flyers at shows and exhibits you attend.
7. Begin a mailing list of friends, acquaintances and other students. Start sending out an interesting newsletter sharing useful information and industry news. Always

include your current class schedule and registration form, making it easy for people to register.

8. Network and participate in quilt-related craft and sewing groups.
9. Join nonquilt-related networking groups and become *visible*.

Teaching Credentials and Qualifications

Do you have a teaching credential to teach elementary or secondary school in your state? If so, include this information prominently in your advertising, resume, business cards and stationery. Do you have a background teaching in local shops, community centers or quilting guilds? If so, add this information. Local teaching experience and training lends credibility to your role as an independent teacher.

Consider teaching certification programs offered by quilting groups such as the National Quilting Association. You may take their course by correspondence over a year's time. When you are ready for your "final," you will meet with three evaluators at a regional or national quilting event. There you will have a personal interview and the handwork you were required to complete in the course assignments will be carefully scrutinized. Once certified, your name will appear on a national registry of quilting teachers. Program chairpersons and organizations use this list to find instructors. Consider national quilting guilds and other organizations that maintain teacher directories. (See chapter ten for addresses.)

Look into teachers' certification programs provided by craft organizations such as the Hobby Industry of America. If you do not have a college degree or you need specific teacher training, look to your state community college system or university for help. Rules and qualifications vary from state to state. California State Universities, for example, provide a program to help you earn a noncredit, adult education teaching credential.

Experienced teachers inspire students to return repeatedly. Prepared teachers who deliver outstanding programs at the state and national level acquire a strong following. Witness the outstanding quilting teachers who travel from one national event to another to find every class they offer is full based upon their reputation alone. Such teachers generate enough enthusiasm that students dispense that most valuable form of advertising—word of mouth. Returning students are even more important to home-based instructors for they form your learning marketplace.

After teaching in my studio, at community colleges and at other guild and local programs, I approached national guilds and organizations offering myself as a freelance teacher. Each assignment led to others. I have traveled to more than half the states in the union to teach crafts at national conventions. I also teach aboard cruise ships—my favorite classroom!

What Do Your Students Want to Learn?

Time for more market research to find out what students want to learn. Stay in touch with local quilting trends in your area. Do most new quilters nearby prefer wearable art, full-sized bed quilts or wall quilts? Have you noted trends toward certain themes—Holidays? Ecological? Victorian? Watercolor or charm quilts? What do newer quilters want to know?

Begin your research by attending as many quilt shows as possible. Listen to comments from observers as you wander through the show. Ask questions of bystanders. Study the quilts that won prizes. Chat with judges or people staffing the show to learn which items created the most interest. Look for quilts that win "People's Choice Awards," for these are a barometer of popular taste.

Return home and organize your information, making a list of four or five class topics you would consider teaching. Begin making quality samples for each class if you don't have them already. Follow the checklist below as you decide what you will offer.

1. Will you teach days, evenings, weekends?
2. What hours will you conduct classes?
3. How long will each session run?
4. How many classes will you offer during each session?
5. How many students can you accommodate comfortably?
6. Will you separate beginners from continuing students or have mixed skill levels?
7. Where will your students buy their supplies? From you? From nearby shops?
8. If buying from a shop, will the owner offer your students discounts for class materials?
9. If you plan to provide materials, will you offer your students a discount?
10. Do you have a class project in mind?
11. Do you have completed samples and some in progress for students to study?
12. Expect a few problem students; we all have them. Prepare to help left-handers and those with limited mobility and flexibility. How will you help slow learners or those who become discouraged easily? Think ahead about how you will deal with argumentative and demanding personalities.

Creating Lesson Plans

After selecting a particular class, begin making a lesson plan. Think of it as a road map to guide you and keep you on track. Students at any level need variation in their class structure. Consider this factor as you break your time into interesting, cohesive segments.

Teaching six or eight students in my home studio differs from my larger college classes. This requires me to maintain two sets of lesson plans for each topic, level and class session.

I've taught knitting, crochet, quilting, needlepoint, embroidery and dressmaking for thirty-three years for California community colleges. Sessions run for eight weeks of three-hour classes each. Bear in mind that I must accept classes of no less than twenty-two students nor more than thirty-five. I could never juggle such large classes without well-organized lesson plans. Keeping them before me during class, I can see at a glance what I have covered and what I must fit into the remaining time.

When I offer the same subject in my home studio, I adjust my guidelines to a two-hour format with far fewer students. To help you tailor your plan based upon classes, students and sessions, see my outline below. I use it as a base to devise a lesson plan for every class. Each three-hour college class offers:

1. Introductory comments for the first session only; questions, answers and comments from the previous class session for subsequent sessions — 15 minutes

2. Demonstrations of new skills, methods and techniques — 45 minutes

3. Show-and-tell of appropriate samples both completed and in progress — 15 minutes

4. Short break so the students can observe my samples closely — 15 minutes

5. Individualized instruction with each student — 60 minutes

6. Book reviews and suggested further reading and research — 5 minutes

7. Formal lecture on a topic related to the lesson or project — 15 minutes

8. Homework assignment and guidelines to complete the work at home — 10 minutes

_____

180 minutes

Naturally, you must allow flexibility. During some classes, you may need to allow more time for one segment, less for another. Now let's put this lesson plan into action using the third class of my sampler quilt-as-you-go session for beginners as a model.

1. Review of last week's block, Rail Fence. Questions? Problems? — 15 minutes

2. Today's block: Ohio Star. Draw schematic on the blackboard.　45 minutes
   a. Define and discuss nine-patch structure and half-squares.
   b. Suggestions for different color treatment.
   c. Have students draft needed templates and check for accuracy.

3. Show visual aid of Ohio Star in progress and two completed　15 minutes
   blocks. One shows perfectly matched points and corners; the
   other shows mismatched corners and intersections. Show
   miniature quilt made with this block plus photos of past
   students' quilts to show the variations possible with different
   color placements.

4. Have a short break so students can examine the samples up　15 minutes
   close.

5. I sit on a chair with rolling wheels, moving from one student　60 minutes
   to the next, answering questions, making suggestions for better
   basting, piecing, pressing. I listen to whatever concerns each
   person.

6. Review two books about sampler quilts. Pass them around to　5 minutes
   students with pages marked that contain Ohio Stars. I
   encourage students to take notes about each pair of books
   reviewed in class so that when the classes end, they have
   become familiar with sixteen quilting books.

7. Formal lecture on fabric grain and bias edges when cutting　15 minutes
   triangles. Tips on how join half-squares and triangles. If time
   allows, students actually cut patches in class.

8. Explain sewing procedure and how to complete Ohio Star. Review　10 minutes
   of basting, backing and quilting lines to complete block by next
   class. To inspire students for the following week, I announce
   which block(s) we will work on at the next class session. I bring
   the sample block, mounted on an easel for preview.

_____

180 minutes = 3 hours

Branching Out

Remember, before you branch out to teach away from home, you must gain teaching
experience and expertise in your speciality locally, and you must learn teaching and
communication skills as well. Enthusiasm and technical ability alone will not qualify
you as a good teacher, especially when teaching away from home.

When you have polished both your craft and teaching skills, consider taking the first step to expanding your position as a quilting teacher. Even if you ultimately plan to teach at national seminars and conferences, start your journey modestly—close by. Practice giving one- or two-day workshops in your home studio or a nearby shop.

Next, branch out into your local community. Offer your classes to local organizations such as art and crafts groups, retired persons' groups, churches, schools and city park and recreation programs. Next, spread out a little farther. Contact quilt guilds nearby and send an informational package about your available classes.

Prepare thoroughly by teaching a "pilot" class to your students before offering it regionally. Pilot classes help you anticipate the type of questions participants will ask as they experience new techniques. This will help you refine lesson plans, visual aids and the organization of your material. You can clarify and revise handouts if necessary. This practice will prepare you to "go on the road."

On the Road

Consider applying to national seminars and conferences after you have gathered experience traveling to nearby groups. This is the perfect time to draw up a specific business plan that will take you from local to national teaching. List both long-term and short-term goals. Set a time line of priorities that will take you where you want to go.

Making Contact

Read quilting magazines and craft trade journals to learn about regional and national seminars or workshops. Contact these groups and send a resume and a list of workshops you have taught, accompanied by brief descriptions. Consider adding your name to teachers' networks such as the *Quilters' Network* or the *National Directory of Professional Quilters*. (Both addresses can be found in chapter ten.)

Groups that find your offerings interesting will invite you to submit a teaching proposal. Many will send you specific guidelines and ready-made forms where you will enter your class information. Others expect you to create your own format. Prepare carefully. Write on letterhead stationery and include your resume, biographical sketch and clips of previously published material if you have them. The time you spend preparing a professional proposal speaks strongly of your competence, organization and credibility.

When a sponsoring group decides to hire you, they usually send a contract that outlines all of the details you need to know, such as:

- The workshop they have chosen
- Date, time and location of the workshop
- Minimum and maximum number of students you will accept
- Level of expertise expected from registrants
- Rate of pay you will receive
- Details about hotel, travel and meals
- The format you must follow to describe your course in the group's program literature
- A materials list and teacher's letter to send to each person who registers for your class

Teachers who travel out-of-state frequently accept one class assignment, then quickly try to add others. Write to groups and quilt guilds near your destination point. Let them know when and where you plan to teach. See if you can book a second class following your first at a destination several miles away. Most groups want to split the travel expenses of a teacher with another group, lowering their cost. However, this can become physically quite tiring for you, so rest adequately between one workshop and the next. Good planning can produce several hundred dollars for a workshop in addition to the goods you may make available for sale.

Most sponsoring groups pass out evaluation sheets to students at the end of the class. Study these carefully, for they offer valuable information about how to improve your class the next time. Here's a last tip you may think is trivial, but it's not. *Never* check your lesson plans and handouts into the cargo hold of a plane. Carry these on board. It's better to replace your clothing or toothbrush than to arrive without your teaching materials, looking unprepared.

About Deductions

Remember, traveling to teach is serious business! All costs for travel, meals and hotels are deductible. Take care to keep good records of your expenses, along with your receipts and invoices. Prepare to collect and pay state sales taxes if you plan to sell supplies.

Make sure you understand the difference between teaching as an independent contractor and teaching as an employee. (The IRS and the books listed in chapter ten define the differences for you.) Courts differentiate an employee from someone with independent status by going over a list of twenty comparison points. The more someone else dictates what you will do, where you will go and how you will work, the more likely it is that you have employee status. If so, you should receive benefits and withholding from your paycheck to cover insurance, state and federal taxes, disability and unemployment insurance.

Independent contractors work for several employers as opposed to just one or two. They work at their own discretion and can accept or reject jobs. They receive a flat amount for services. Nothing is withheld from their paychecks. Become informed on this troublesome issue so you will know and understand your status.

If you manage your teaching business according to IRS standards of profit making, *all* of your expenses are deductible. Run it casually without records and accurate bookkeeping, and you may find that the IRS can label you as a "hobbyist" not intent on making a profit. Under audit, you may have your deductions disallowed and find yourself owing back taxes and penalties—something you will want to avoid at all costs.

Teaching by Correspondence

Quilting teachers, why not add to your income by teaching correspondence courses? Some people prefer to learn at their own pace by mail. Those who study at home need instructors. You have an advantage if you have already been teaching quilting—you already have organized lesson plans in place.

Begin by writing a comprehensive course outline describing the content of your complete course. Explain everything you plan to include. Next, convert all of your usual oral instructions into written form. Arrange your material so that students learn in a logical, sensible order, and then group the information into lessons. Decide how many lessons it takes to offer the student a rich, educational experience. Be specific about what each person will learn from your course. It may take months to complete a good correspondence course, but once done, all you need to do is make copies of your material each time you take on a new student.

After completing the description and contents of your course, break the information into lessons. Students need to see ideas flowing from one lesson to the next. Before adding new techniques, show how they relate to previously learned material.

Teaching by correspondence differs from personal teaching in a critical aspect. You will not be physically present to determine whether your students have understood your information. I have solved this by preparing homework essay questions that appear at the end of each lesson. Stick to questions that cannot be answered with a simple "yes" or "no." Below you will find a few examples of essay questions from one of my lessons:

1. Have you ever appliquéd before? If so, please describe. If not, why not?
2. If you have tried appliqué before, what did you find the most difficult to do? What was easiest?
3. What particular books or patterns do you have about appliqué?
4. Why do you want to learn more about appliqué now? What do you hope to gain?
5. Do you have a specific project in mind that requires appliqué?
6. Did you find my instructions easy to understand? If not, what would have made them easier for you to follow?

Make sure your questions and assignments cause students to research information. I include a book list with each lesson inviting students to comment on which ones they have read.

When everything is in place, begin thinking about how to market your course. Determine which magazines and journals your potential students might read. Select from these to place your first classified ads.

Record keeping becomes important as soon as students begin to enroll. I begin a file folder for each person and maintain details of his or her progress. I make copies of all of the correspondence we exchange. Here is the system I use:

- Each time a student completes and returns a lesson to me, I study it carefully, adding corrections and suggestions as needed.
- I make photocopies of all the materials the student has enclosed.
- For recording progress on actual quilting samples, I also use my photocopy machine. Though it does not produce color, it does preserve a reminder of each person's workmanship and submissions.
- After recording all of the new information in each student's file, I return the corrected lesson to the student and add the materials for the next lesson.

I researched the potential of teaching by correspondence before I began. Students who had studied by correspondence before agreed that unexplained delays getting their lessons and samples returned to them topped their list of complaints. This information helped me decide immediately how to position myself in the marketplace. All of my correspondence classes come with a guarantee that I will *always* respond within two weeks—no excuses.

Wise teachers know they will learn the most from their own students. Keep an open mind to new ideas from all sources and learn as you teach.

CHAPTER 7 CHECKLIST

✓ Teaching from home can be challenging, requiring careful time management and, oftentimes, adaptive strategies.

✓ If you do not have teaching credentials, consider certification programs from quilting and other craft organizations. It will help your credibility.

✓ Research your geographical area carefully to determine what to charge for your classes. Pricing information is readily available if you know where to look. Study the system provided on page 114 and modify it to suit your needs, geographical area and quilting specialty. Only you can determine how much you want to earn, but there are many guidelines to help you find the perfect system.

✓ Finding students is the marketing task of all home-based teachers. Take time to do your homework. Do all that you can to motivate students to return for more.

✓ Lesson plans are the heart of teaching. Take time to organize and plan well. Students are quick to criticize an unorganized instructor but always praise one whose lessons show preparation.

✓ Once you've gathered teaching experience locally, look to expand your horizons but proceed with caution, growing slowly and steadily.

✓ Regional and national teaching require extensive preparation and experience. Make sure you're ready before you apply, but once you are accepted to teach at national conferences and conventions, you've arrived as a quilting teacher.

✓ Think about teaching by correspondence from your home office, especially if you live in a rural area. Though it takes a lot of paperwork and organization, it's both profitable and satisfying.

KAREN COMBS—
QUILT TEACHER
AND WRITER

PHOTO BY GLAMOUR SHOTS

Designing her own quilts inspired Karen Combs to want to teach. She couldn't wait to share her knowledge and enthusiasm with others. Says Karen, "I began living and breathing quilts in 1973 while still in high school, but teaching quilting became my dream. Then, I reasoned, I could legitimately surround myself with fabric, books, notions and sewing machines (I have three!). I would also have the perfect excuse to attend all quilt shows within driving distance. I wanted to soak up quilting information and share it with others."

Though Karen quilted occasionally for the next few years, it was not until she left her full-time job to care for her children that she had enough time to quilt seriously.

Karen's dream came true in 1989 when she began to teach quilting for a community education program. She also began writing articles for quilting magazines.

Living in the Midwest most of her life, everything changed for Karen in 1990 when her husband was transferred to a southern state six hundred miles away. By then, Karen felt committed to teaching. As soon as her family settled in their new home, "I hit the ground running," declares Karen. "I discovered the nearest guild was fifty miles away. Within a month, I began teaching classes in the local art center of our town and helped to start a new quilt guild closer to home."

Karen credits quilting activities with helping her adjust to a different state, climate and culture in record time. Quilting brought her immediate friends with whom she shared her quilting interests.

Within a year, Karen branched out, teaching for quilt guilds, shows and retreats. Meanwhile, she continued to write and publish more articles for such well-known quilt magazines as *Quilter's Newsletter, Traditional Quilter, International Quilter* and *Lady's Circle Patchwork Quilts.* Her article titled "Transparency," in the September 1996 issue of *Quilter's Newsletter,* attests to her skills as a colorist as well as a teacher.

Karen discovered that to teach at a local level, one must diversify. She learned to teach many types of quilting methods utilizing a variety of designs and patterns. However, when traveling away from home to teach at shows and guilds, she wanted to specialize. "I love quilts that create optical illusions," says Karen. "Today, students recognize this as my specialty.

"Several reasons keep me going," admits Karen. "The most important is that I love what I do. Nothing excites me more than planning for the next quilting class, designing a new project, writing a new article or packing for the next quilt show. I love

sharing my knowledge with others and want to encourage people to try new ideas or techniques.

Karen's children presently attend junior high and high school, so she knows college tuition expenses will begin in a few years. Karen feels fortunate that although she must teach for financial reasons, she is fortunate to have a job she loves.

"Teaching enables me to travel (which I love to do), meet people and have experiences I never would have had otherwise," says Karen. "I have traveled across the country by myself, developed friendships with quilters while staying in their homes and developed confidence to stand in front of a roomful of students."

Karen feels it is important to have a sense of humor when teaching. "Students like to have fun in class and they like a teacher who enjoys herself. I need a sense of humor because students often express surprise when they meet me for the first time. They expect a quilt teacher who teaches nationwide to be a . . . well, little old lady." Students in Karen's classes often comment that although she is in her late thirties, she looks too young to be teaching at a nationwide level. At times, they also express uncer-

tainty that they can learn from someone who looks so young. Karen handles those situations with humor, packing her classes with even more information. "Many times after a class, students approach me and say, 'I learned so much and I had fun too.' "

Karen takes her quilting business seriously. She has developed brochures, business cards and letterhead to portray herself as a professional who takes pride in her career.

Often teachers feel they do not need to market their businesses in the same way that others who sell products do. Karen shows her wisdom in recognizing this error and markets her classes and lectures in several ways. To market herself as a professional instructor, Karen's name appears in several quilting teachers' lists. She appears on the rosters of the Tennessee Valley Quilt Association, the Kentucky Heritage Quilt Society, the Interstate Regional Quilters Network and the National Directory of Professional Quilters, to name a few.

Karen also markets her teaching services after a class ends. "When I teach away from home, I always bring brochures. At the end of classes, I ask if anyone wants information about my other classes. Students can then return home and pass my information to their local program chairpersons. Word of mouth is one of the best ways to market. When guild participants like you and your classes, they share the information with other guilds, even at a national level.

"Last year I placed an ad in the classified section of several quilting magazines describing my quilting classes. I found several teaching jobs from the ad, thus the cost was worthwhile."

Writing continues to be important to Karen. She chooses to write and publish articles to share her knowledge and to create interest in the classes and techniques she offers. Karen is currently writing her first book, entitled *Master of Illusions: Optical Illusions for Quilters*, which will be published by the American Quilter's Society.

"Quilting often changes the life of the women it touches," says Karen. "It develops self-confidence for students and provides them with a sense of accomplishment. I am proud to be a small part of these transformations."

KAREN COMBS

1405 Creekview Court, Columbia, TN 38401

Phone:

(615) 380-0081

E-mail:

KCOMBS1004@aol.com

CHAPTER EIGHT

MORE WAYS TO MAKE MONEY

Selling handmade quilts is not the only way to *Make Your Quilting Pay for Itself.* This chapter offers you many more options.

Consulting: How to Rent Your Expertise by the Hour

Consultants of all types receive payment by sharing their knowledge and resources by the hour. Professionals such as doctors, lawyers, accountants, financial planners and small business consultants make their living this way. Why not you? Even if you offer consulting services only occasionally, they provide additional income tied to your quilting expertise.

Polish up your promotional documents as your first step. Make sure your brochures, resume and flyers make the impression that you are a professional and take your business seriously. Listing the services you can provide to clients on your brochure is also a good idea.

A Consulting Model

Let's study the marketing procedures often used by interior decorators, who also sell creative advice to others. The model below applies to quilters as well. Here are a few ideas:

• Offer to choose colors and to lay out original designs for those expert quilters who lack confidence in design. You can even visit these clients in their own homes to get an idea of the look they are trying to achieve.

• Affiliate yourself with local interior decorators and offer to design (or make) quilts and home decorating items for their clients' homes. If satisfied, such decorators may bring more custom work to you from other clients.

• Offer to make "house calls" to help others solve quilting problems. A group of women I know specialize in authenticating and dating old quilts. They have sources for older fabrics and have acquired a high level of repair and restoration skills they teach to others. They can match old colors and fabrics to restore old treasures.

Identify Your Expertise

Begin by defining the exact services you can deliver. This will help you recognize the clients who can benefit from your expertise. Successful consultants always remain aware of their clients' needs. Giving clients what they want and need is the hallmark of successful consultants.

Marketing my consulting practice was easier than I thought.

• First, I added a paragraph describing my consulting practice in my brochure.

• I revised the text using the same information in my yellow pages ad in the local directory. A phone company representative actually called me after receiving my revision. She told me the ad would appear in the consulting section of the phone directory at no extra cost to me since it was a natural cross-reference.

• I designed a one-page flyer describing exactly what I could offer clients and added it to the literature I make available to anyone who writes or calls seeking information about my services.

Below you will find fourteen tips and ideas gleaned from my own consulting practice. Perhaps they will get you thinking.

1. Begin with a contract. Specify what services you can offer your clients and what clients can expect from you. If you need help creating contracts, refer to the book, *Simple Contracts*, by attorney Stephen Elias and Marcia Stewart (also listed in chapter ten).

2. Find out what other consultants charge in your community. Generally, consultants charge by the hour or job. Research carefully to learn how to set up a realistic fee schedule. (Review chapter seven for more about setting fees.)

3. When selling advice, good consultants do not guarantee that it will result in specific profits or results. Make it clear that while you offer resources, direction and suggestions, clients must implement your ideas. How they utilize your information becomes their responsibility and success or failure depends upon their own efforts.

4. When potential clients contact you, listen as they talk to you by phone or in person. Take written notes about their needs and questions.

5. Determine their principal reason for calling as soon as possible. Ask specific

questions. Learn exactly what the client needs. Listen while they describe their problems and frustrations.

6. Prepare thoroughly before meeting with a client for the first time. Research all that you can about their specific interests.

7. State your hourly fee and set a mutually convenient time when you can meet.

8. Suggest to clients that they prepare for the visit with a *written* list of questions.

9. Provide each client with a suggested reading list including all practical resources you can find. Clients like to receive tangible, written material to take away with them.

10. Remember that clients pay for your exclusive attention. Discourage small talk and stick to issues important to them.

11. Listen attentively. Clients often want to put their ideas, priorities and goals into words to sort out their own thinking.

12. Take time to refer your clients to other resources that can help them add to the information you have provided them, such as teachers, quilting associations, seminars and guilds. Include upcoming local events such as meetings and fairs to enable your clients to continue their learning experiences.

13. Some clients may benefit from a list of manufacturers, distributors and sales representatives as well.

14. Last, consider disconnecting your phones during the entire period you are meeting with a client so you will not be interrupted. Housemates and children should respect your time with a client and not intrude. Those who pay for your time have a right to expect and receive your undivided attention.

If you decide to pursue consulting seriously, you will find three books on the subject listed in the chapter ten. Jeffrey Lant, the author of two of these books says, "Don't *give* someone a piece of your mind. Sell it to them." His books helped me establish myself as a small business consultant to crafters of all types, adding substantially to my yearly income.

Have You Tried Demonstrating?

"If crafts and hobbies are your business . . . Hobby Industry Association (HIA) is the association with the tools and connections you need!" So states the HIA brochure. Slogans such as this often prove themselves to be overstated, but with HIA, every word is true.

Quilting may be a hobby for millions of consumers but for those of us who choose it as a business, HIA has much to offer. "But I thought HIA serves florists, decorative painters and jewelry crafters, not quilters," you may say. One breathtaking visit to an HIA annual convention disproves this common misconception. Indeed, HIA has much to offer professional quilters. I'll discuss more about HIA in the next chapter, but for now, let's focus on their program for professional demonstrators—an excellent way to make extra money.

HIA's Training Program

HIA's Certified Professional Demonstrator training program teaches craft experts in every speciality, including quilting, to give polished product demonstrations to consumers. Whether in your hometown quilting shop, in a TV studio or at a national convention, you can get paid to showcase products you use regularly.

Begin to consider this idea by attending an annual HIA Convention. Walk around the show floor of over 3,000 product booths (gasp!) and observe. Stop and watch a few booth demonstrators as they explain product benefits to onlookers. Afterward, locate a few booths where they sell quilting supplies. Observe again. How does the booth look? Is the demonstrator explaining a product unfamiliar to you or have you used it before? Is the demonstrator including information on new techniques? Do other onlookers seem attentive to the speaker? Are they asking and receiving answers to questions? Good demonstrations include some hands-on opportunities. Try the product if feasible. How are other onlookers faring as they experiment?

Can you see yourself behind the table talking about one of your favorite topics—quilt supplies? If so, contact the HIA show office. They will direct you to meetings set up to train new product demonstrators. Make an effort to go. I have seen several friends and acquaintances go from the meeting directly to a booth of their choice.

If this sounds good to you, choose a company that sells products you are familiar with. Present yourself as a novice demonstrator at their booth area and ask if you can observe their people demonstrating, then give a demonstration yourself. Though you will not be paid for this initial "practice run," you will get an idea if this activity suits you, and company owners will get the chance to watch you in action. Many companies actually hire new demonstrators this way and offer them additional training.

Industry giants such as HIA offer a Certified Craft Demonstrator program. You will learn how to demonstrate sewing and quilt-related products and notions in shops and industry events across the country.

With the support of HIA, manufacturers call you to showcase their products to both consumer and trade groups. You can travel as far as you want. Techniques that you can demonstrate to others include how to:

- Use a rotary cutter
- Use stencil cremes and textile paints to create quilting designs
- Fuse and bond adhesive papers to fabric
- Make templates
- Set up a quilt floor or lap frame
- Trace designs to be hand-quilted or machine-quilted later
- Use a specific type of thimble to demonstrate hand-quilting
- Quilt by machine

HIA follows up and supports their demonstrators by sending regularly updated information, audio tapes and newsletters specifically for demonstrators. They will explain the certification procedure to you. If you opt for certification and pass the simple requirements, your name will appear in the HIA registry as a professional demonstrator.

Manufacturers have confidence that HIA-trained demonstrators will show their products effectively. They use the registry to hire you directly as they prepare to promote a specific product at shows around the country. You also have the option of applying to such companies directly and offering your services.

For example, you may find yourself showing consumers how to use the latest fusibles at your local craft chain store or how to trace a quilting pattern on a modern light table at a local quilt show. You will receive payment for each presentation.

Defray travel expenses when you attend national conventions and seminars. Show participants how to use the latest quilter's tools during a show, for example. Many demonstrators establish permanent business relationships with specific manufacturers, representing them several times each year. Why not consider developing an ongoing liaison with the supplier of your favorite quilting tools and materials?

If this idea sounds interesting, first complete your certification training. After that, scan trade show books and trade journals for the names and addresses of companies that produce quilt-related products. Send them a brief, well-written letter expressing your interest in demonstrating for them. Give the date, place and specific event that you wish to attend. Naturally, mention your certification credentials. Close by stating that you will follow up in a week or two with a phone call to see if you can be of service. If you have previous demonstrator experience, say so. Ask someone to photograph you as you are demonstrating so you can send a copy to each company you contact in the future. There is no industry standard about payment as there are so many variables. Some demonstrators receive a check after the event but in other cases, the company may opt to pay for your hotel stay, defray your travel expenses or pay you in complimentary supplies. All details are negotiable.

Working With Other Quilters

Offering your services to established, busy, successful quilters provides another profit-making option. You may cut, sew or hand-quilt for teachers and other professionals who need another pair of hands. Consider completing quilts or quilting by the hour for quilt artists who must go on to other projects.

You may also advertise and furnish your services to other quilters who may not wish to complete their own quilted projects or who need help. Study Karen Brown's profile at the end of this chapter. See how she established a machine quilting service by completing the quilts of students and friends.

You can hand- or machine-quilt for customers or quilt to order! Complete the unfinished projects of others or mend, restore or embellish. A quilter I know will visit a home and mount and baste a quilt top to a frame, leaving the remaining hand-quilting process to the owner.

How do you find quilters who need your service? By advertising. Think about using a two-pronged approach. Place a classified ad in your local newspaper to reach people in your community. Place a second ad in one or more of your favorite quilting magazines to reach quilters across the country. Even those who quilt regularly may prefer to do some of their own work and hire someone else to complete it.

Distribute flyers whenever possible. Enter local and regional quilt shows and show your best work. Make sure others have access to your literature outlining what you can do for them. Press releases sent to newspapers always generate interest. The first time you complete a quilt with an interesting story, perhaps an antique top someone inherited, invite your local newspaper to cover the story with pictures. This will send you on your way.

Talk About Quilting

Think of public speaking not as a fearsome experience, but as an opportunity to share what you know and love about quilting. Recall a few of the interesting speakers you have heard in the past. Harriet Hargrave can talk about any quilt-related subject whatsoever and mesmerizes her audience. Helen Kelley's work with appliqué and her marvelous postage stamp quilts keep everyone awestruck. Quilters everywhere agree that Mary Ellen Hopkins makes them laugh at her wit and themselves.

These professional speakers and expert quilters have a wealth of information to share. Where do you fit in? Remember, these three popular, in-demand quilting speakers and many others started small once upon a time. They were not born and labeled "famous quilters" from childhood. They worked hard, learned and persisted, and so must you.

How to Start Speaking in Public

Public speaking strikes fear in the hearts of some. If you feel apprehensive, join your local Toastmaster's group. Scan your local papers for names of program chairpersons of various community organizations—not only quilt- or fiber-related groups. Obtain a list of local organizations and their program chairs from your Chamber of Commerce office. Send each organization you find of interest an informational, professional package describing what you have to offer.

Write to the program chairpersons on your letterhead stationery and include your brochure and business card. Sell them on the idea of paying you for an upcoming "program" for their members. For example, I've presented show-and-tell "trunk shows" for parents' nursery school groups, hospital volunteer groups, a group of oil painters, church groups and 4-H programs.

While you may begin by providing such programs for just experience and no pay, you can gradually begin to request a small honorarium of say $25 to $50. Read the books on the subject in chapter ten, then start small. Begin by offfering to do a show-and-tell for your church, school or social group. After you gather experience, you can move on to other local groups that you do not know. Put together slide presentations and programs about your passion. Gather the best examples of your work into a "trunk show."

Give more than 100 percent at each opportunity and word will get out that you, too, are worth listening to. Remember this: Try to inspire, entertain, educate and motivate your audiences. Grow gradually and you may find that public speaking engagements can add welcome, additional profit to your quilting business.

CHAPTER 8 CHECKLIST

✓ Consulting is nothing more than sharing your ideas, resources and skills for a fee. When you think of yourself as a professional, realize you have information for sale that others want.

✓ Getting paid to give demonstrations using products you love can be profitable. Not only can you defray travel expenses to seminars and conferences, but if you become listed in HIA's registry of demonstrators, local shops and manufacturers will call upon you as needed.

✓ Working with and for other quilters is yet another way to profit from your quilting skills. Doing so will also widen your quilting network.

✓ Consider giving programs about quilting at guild meetings. Gradually polish and add to your presentations. Why not get paid to share what you know?

✓ If you decide to earn money from your quilting and if you're like the rest of us, you'll learn that you will probably need to undertake several profitable activities to earn what you want. Seldom do quilt professionals stick to one endeavor exclusively. Even with part-time work, you'll undoubtedly need to wear more than one hat to generate the income you need.

KAREN BROWN—
MACHINE
QUILTING . . . AT
YOUR SERVICE

Quilting became Karen Brown's passion only seven years ago. Before then, she had made three quilts using her grandmother's traditional methods, which was all she knew at that time. Karen merely cut squares, pieced them together and tied the quilt with yarn rather than hand-quilting.

Everything changed for Karen in 1989. Home from work for a few days, she happened to turn on her TV to see a demonstration about how to make a Pineapple design quilt. "Boy, that really looks easy!" she thought and immediately began shopping for quilting books. Overnight, Karen became a fabric addict. When shops offered 40 percent or 50 percent off of their regular prices on fabric, Karen added to her stash. For the next two years, she made many quilts and took her first quilting classes.

Working a forty-hour week didn't leave Karen much time to hand-quilt, so she turned to machine quilting. Says Karen, "I bought books about machine quilting, found a walking foot for my old Singer and taught myself to do straight-line and stitch-in-the-ditch machine quilting.

Wow! That helped me pump out those quilts!''

In 1992, Karen took a machine quilting class at a local high school and learned freehand quilting, cross hatching and appliqué. Understanding the new techniques excited her, but she still had very little time to practice. Karen made a new quilting friend in the class who had studied the ''Make-a-Quilt-in-a-Day'' books written by Eleanor Burns. Together, Karen and her friend signed up for a teacher training class in San Marcos, California, sponsored by the publishers of the quilt-in-a-day books. Though her friend had to cancel at the last moment, Karen still went by herself. She acknowledges that the week-long course greatly contributed to preparing her to teach quilting and sewing techniques to others.

''Teaching was not my goal at the time, but I thought the class would provide detailed instruction and it did. By the end of the week, I found myself thinking that perhaps I could teach after all. As long as I was spending *all* my spare time quilting, I should be earning some money, but how? Should I open a quilt shop, teach classes, make custom quilts or what?'' pondered Karen.

Friends who admired Karen's quilts wanted her to make quilts for them but she decided to teach them to make their own. Since Karen works for a community college, she decided to offer a *free* class to test the market.

Karen next made a decisive move. She obtained a seller's permit enabling her to buy quilting supplies, tools and books at wholesale to sell to her students. Though Karen had not expected to make a profit, her class was successful and she generated income as well.

''That fall,'' adds Karen, ''I learned that a fabric chain store nearby needed a quilt teacher. I applied and got the job! I continued teaching there for two years and still sold supplies to students as the store didn't stock the items I preferred.''

Students returned for more, increasing the demand for her classes. Karen received a discount on her purchases but admits she spent her earnings buying more fabric.

Karen made and quilted more than twenty quilts during her first year of teaching. She began thinking about buying an industrial quilting machine but found that the prices were too high.

Then a classified ad caught Karen's eye. She read about a used quilting machine for sale at $4,250. With her husband's approval, she invested in a Nolting 24-inch Long Arm Quilter.

Since the machine rests on a 14-foot, one-piece table, it became obvious that they were going to have a challenge getting it into the basement. ''We had adequate space in the basement, but with a four-level home and many corners to manage, trying to reach the basement seemed impossible,'' explains Karen. Her third-level hallway dead ends into storage cabinets and is then followed by a sharp turn to enter the garage. Karen explains the solution to the problem. ''My husband cut a hole in the drywall on the garage side, slipped the table through the hole and through the storage cabinets, and voilá—a straight shot to the basement!''

Afterward, Karen realized she needed instruction to learn how to use her newfound treasure. She signed up to attend a special class in Minnesota and with her son's frequent flyer ticket in hand, off she went.

''The class proved invaluable in helping me start the business I have today,'' says Karen. ''I learned how to position a quilt on the machine and exactly what the machine could do.''

Next, Karen found herself

practicing more. Frustration ensued due to inadequate time to practice to acquire the confidence she wanted. She planned to quilt several of her own quilt tops before quilting for others, but students began bringing Karen *their* quilts. At times, she admits, she had to rip out stitches but learned much in the process.

"I bought the machine in June and quit teaching at the fabric store in December. Having a seller's permit and business cards, I requested catalogs to buy wholesale supplies such as thread and batting for my business. Teaching already supported my habit, but now my part-time quilting business generated more income."

Like many of us, the Internet beckoned to Karen. She joined a quilt business list and placed a small ad on their home page to advertise her machine quilting services. Karen's first order came from Houston. Soon after completing that quilt, three more quilt tops arrived plus recommendations of her work to other quilters. Karen continues to receive frequent inquiries from the ad while former students still bring her their quilt tops.

"I advertise on the World Wide Web," Karen explains. "But in my hometown, my only advertising is word of mouth." Since Karen still only quilts part time, she always has enough work but not the time to quilt for herself.

However, this may change. Karen and her husband have discussed her doing machine quilting full time, but for the moment, her day job pays well and provides benefits. Says Karen, "For now, my machine quilting income pays for all of my supplies and leaves me a little extra to feed my fabric habit. I am happy!"

KAREN BROWN: QUILT CREATIONS

27512 N. Bear Lake Road, Chattaroy, WA 99003

Phone:

(509) 238-4348

Fax:

(509) 238-6030

E-mail:

kbrown@iea.com

KEEP LEARNING

Questioning what you already know keeps you vital and interesting. New information stimulates your brain and creativity. Remaining informed becomes even more important when you want to profit from your knowledge. Quilt professionals must continually broaden their technical skills while keeping up with what goes on in the field. Don't settle for only quilt-specific information. You also must keep in touch with crafts in general, economic issues and the external marketplace. "But how?" you ask. By networking!

Networking

Networking means the informal sharing of information among individuals or groups who are linked by a common interest. Today, it has become a buzzword critical to everyone who wants to get ahead in any business, large or small, part-time or full-time.

Quilt hobbyists enjoy getting together to share techniques and to admire each other's work. After all, this is the primary function of quilt guilds. Quilt professionals, however, must go beyond quilting on a social level. Networking with others in the field allows you to develop professional contacts and to share manufacturer and product information, such as wholesale sources, marketing trends, teaching opportunies and upcoming trade shows. How do you participate?

How Networking Works

Networking can take place at guild meetings, shops, classes and conventions. At first it may sound like conversation. However, if you listen carefully, rather than hearing small talk shifting from one subject to another, you'll find that networking remains focused on a specific topic.

Participate by asking questions and listening attentively. When someone needs information you have, share it. Networking at conferences and conventions invites an even more avid discussion of common goals, ideas and problems.

Participants introduce themselves and then respond to previously agreed upon issues common to them. Think of networking as playing two roles simultaneously—that of teacher and student. Take pains to avoid a common networking pitfall: It is not fair to drain others of information and provide none yourself. Exchanging freely and equally characterizes good networking. Where do you start?

Quilting and Craft Organizations

Join local, regional and national organizations where quilters and other crafters gather. Quilting organizations address quilting issues and provide continuing education in the field. Groups such as HIA and SCD will help you see the business of quilting within a craft context. All of the above groups along with many others provide regular conferences and seminars, giving professionals the opportunity to exchange ideas and to meet others in their field to discuss common concerns.

Let's start with the two primary organizations for quilters, the National Quilting Association (NQA) and the American Quilting Society (AQS). (You will find their addresses in the next chapter.) Both groups publish quarterly magazines to keep serious quilters up-to-date on the status of quilting. NQA maintains a teacher directory of members they have certified. Join one or both of these organizations to learn:

- What respected teachers have to say
- Which quilt styles and designs are in vogue
- About the latest quilt books and newsletters
- About the latest quilt tools and other related products
- The location of shows, exhibits and workshops across the country.

Next, consider joining a nonquilt-specific craft organization. Their seminars and publications will help keep you informed about the entire craft market of which quilting is a part. You must know how quilting fits into the crafts world—needlework and sewing in particular. A list of these organizations and their addresses appears in the next chapter. For now, let's take an in-depth look at two national organizations I find most valuable. Membership in both has propelled my quilting business forward.

The Society of Craft Designers

The Society of Craft Designers (SCD) provides an annual seminar at varying locations where its members meet and network with magazine editors from most of the craft magazines. Editors scrutinize the latest craft designs, including quilting, to become familiar with the work of designers and to buy their latest creations. Designers may meet up to twenty editors during the seminar, with each meeting offering a potential sale or design assignment. I have sold quilt designs to the editors of *Crafts Magazine, Quilt Craft* and *Lady's Circle Patchwork Quilts* while attendng SCD seminars.

During the seminars, SCD-established designers share their knowledge of the industry. Each year, editors from different craft magazines explain what they need to fill the pages of their magazines. They always describe what is *not* selling and what colors, products and styles to avoid. Color and trend experts share their expertise and forecast colors for the upcoming season. Manufacturers fill meeting rooms with the latest supplies. Tables arrayed with countless complimentary products invite exploration by designers for their future designing year.

What does this mean to the average quilt designer? Opportunity! Many designers receive enough assignments to keep them producing all year. Editors find exactly the designs they want to publish, and designers gain the security of knowing that completed projects have a ready buyer.

SCD publishes a bimonthly newsletter and *Who's Who in Crafts*, a directory of members cross-referenced by specialty and state. Manufacturers, editors and publishers who are looking for quilters or other craft specialists refer to this directory. One company introducing a line of quilting thread contacted me and other quilt designers. They generously sent spools of all their colors and invited us to experiment. Each participant who submitted their quilting samples using this product received a lovely sewing basket filled with even more samples. Several of us received invitations to submit a specific design for their upcoming promotions.

SCD provided the opportunity for me to try many products for the first time. I learned how to use stencil cremes on my quilts at an SCD seminar. After receiving stencils and cremes, I designed a quilt combining stenciling with Trapunto quilting and sold the design to *Crafts Magazine* within three months. I also received samples of different battings, quilting threads, fabric adhesives and textile paints from all major companies.

Review chapter six for other SCD membership benefits such as design assignments, endorsement fees and complimentary supplies. Considering the benefits described above, members agree that networking at seminars is the most valuable aspect of SCD membership. (SCD's address is found in the next chapter.)

The Hobby Industry Association

The Hobby Industry Association (HIA) is the largest craft organization in the *world*. This organization of 3,600 companies and individuals supports the craft industry of which quilting is a part. The membership list includes:

- Manufacturers
- Wholesalers, including fabric, thread, sewing and quilting supply companies
- Manufacturer representatives, who can create new markets for your quilted items
- Trade and consumer publishers
- Professional craft producers. Those of you who mass-produce quilts and related items for sale will find a strong, growing network of talented artisans who make a career selling what they make
- Service suppliers, including quilting teachers and designers

Professional training programs continue as the prime HIA service. See chapters four and eight for details about HIA's Certified Teacher Training and Certified Professional Demonstrator programs.

Here's another HIA benefit for quilters. Manufacturers offer dozens of hands-on workshops to its members during conventions. From brief "make-it, take-it" experiences to in-depth classes, members learn how to use the latest products. Manufacturers and their staffs, experts in developing products, show you how to use them. You don't think this applies to quilters? Think again!

Below you will find a list of workshops of interest to quilters that were offered during a recent HIA convention. Classes are free except for a modest registration fee of $7 per class.

1. Ribbon flowers and yo-yo appliqués on chambray vests
2. Cross-stitch on noncounted fabrics
3. Beaded embroidery on crazy quilts
4. Watercolor painting on fabric
5. Fabric floral painting
6. Silk ribbon embroidery
7. Punch quilting
8. Ribbon embellishments
9. Battenburg lace embellishment
10. Painting on silk
11. Rubber stamping on fabric

Do not expect HIA to offer in-depth, all-day quilting workshops. Choose national or regional quilting conventions and seminars for quilt-specific classes. Attending HIA's convention, however, does permit you to see the latest fabrics, notions, threads and tools for quilting and how quilting fits in with other crafts. Why not design your next quilt for sale based upon the latest trends in color, subject matter or style? Here are other HIA benefits:

- Since quilts take a long time to make, you will receive a head start on design and color trends. During each convention, you can attend panel discussions and listen to editors of prime magazines tell you what's hot and what's not. Each year, editors from magazines such as *McCall's Needlework, Sew News, McCall's Quilting* and *Crafts Magazine* inform participants of industry trends.
- If you already quilt professionally, HIA's annual survey will help you decide about how and where to advertise effectively.
- If you sell quilting items or literature, you learn what consumers want and what they are currently buying.
- As a teacher, you can plan classes around consumer's preferences and promote timely techniques.

My list of important networking, educational and marketing opportunities would not be complete without another mention of Karey Bresenhan's vital quilting event, the International Quilt Festival/Market. Refer to the introduction for more about the only wholesale trade show in the world for the quilting and soft crafts industry.

Expand your personal network of business contacts and organizations if you want to profit from your quilting. Though quilters generally work in solitude, you cannot succeed in business alone. Networking offers continual sources of information, ideas and additional contacts that help keep you profitable.

As you can see from this book, countless opportunities exist to support, advise and educate hard-working quilters and other crafters, thus helping them to succeed.

CHAPTER 9 CHECKLIST

✓ Networking experiences are critical to professional quilters. Never underestimate their value. Question everyone around you and be generous with your own information.

✓ Join both quilting and nonquilt-specific craft organizations. Membership provides continuous, fresh, updated information and helps you get ahead. The groups mentioned in this chapter are but a few of the many excellent choices you have.

✓ Most quilters who profit from their skills agree that at least one visit to the International Quilt Festival/Market in Houston is a must. The exposure, stimulation and opportunities are absolutely overwhelming. Before starting a quilting business of any kind, you owe it to yourself to see your ideas in perspective. Go!

Barbara Barrick McKie—A Multi-Talented Quilter

Barbara (Barb) Barrick McKie began her working life in 1963, not as a quilter, but as a research scientist for the Eli Lilly Corporation. While home for several years with her first child, Barb had time to begin a second career as a seamstress and professional quilter. She then became a computer consultant and finally, she entered marketing management. Today, this talented lady has combined all of the above into her present career as an art quilter with a related computer business on the side.

"Sewing had always appealed to me," says Barb. "I had always sewn my own clothes, including my graduation dress from high school and my bridal gown. I met my future business partner when I volunteered to make costumes for a local production of *Show Boat*. She was the costume designer, and I sewed many of the costumes. We were both impressed with each other's talents, so in 1971, I left my work as a scientist and, with my partner, started a sewing business.

"First, we made clothing for children, which lead us to design lingerie for little girls that we sold to Saks 5th Avenue. There wasn't enough profit margin, so we decided to enter the more lucrative field of making bridal gowns, which proved successful. However, the repetitive sewing of the same designs and competition from cheap overseas labor wore us out and our interest waned."

Barb had learned to quilt from her grandmother in earlier years, but in 1971 she renewed her interest with great enthusiasm when she and her husband purchased their first home. She decided to fill the four-bedroom house with bed and wall quilts. She explains that her passion for quilting developed from her love of sewing.

Barb went on to display her quilts in the Guildford, Connecticut, Handcraft Show, which led to several commissions. She soon met other local quilters and organized a group show, which proved to be financially very successful.

"Seventeen of my early quilts

appeared in emerging quilt books of the day," says Barb. Though her earnings provided her with all of the cash she needed to pay for her growing stash of fabric, she yearned to expand both her computer and quilt interests to increase her income.

Barb decided to try her hand at making and selling custom-designed art quilts through galleries. She knew she did not want to make duplicate items as she had in the bridal business. Drawing from her experience with organizing and presenting herself in a businesslike manner to clients and galleries, she recognized she needed more education to market her quilts.

"My sewing business inspired me to learn more about what it takes to have a successful enterprise," says Barb. "I gave up my bridal business in 1982 and turned to another interest—computers." Barb worked as a computer consultant for the next ten years but maintained her enthusiasm for quilting. In 1992, Barb went back to school and received her M.S. degree in marketing management, planning to put her new skills to use in her own quilting business.

Barb never regretted her decision. She goes on to explain, "I liked communications and computer consulting and learned that marketing was the best way to make wise business direction choices and to communicate clearly with others. Unexpectedly, in 1993, I was offered a job as marketing manager for the nondegree computer education courses at the Hartford Graduate Center where I had gotten my degree. My job was just like running a small business. I made decisions as to which courses to offer, developed marketing materials such as brochures and ads, and hired and managed teachers and administrative employees.

"Since I had been the photography and engravings editor for high school and college yearbooks respectively, it was a natural to work with the printers, desktop publishing people and photographers in developing the marketing materials."

Meanwhile, in 1991, both Barb and her husband developed an interest in genealogy, which requires intense research into family history. "I decided to capture my family's history by making a genealogical quilt," explains Barb, "but I realized I had to buy computer and heat press equipment to achieve the image transfer quality and flexibility I wanted." Barb continued to study different methods for transferring photographic and other images to fabric, intrigued with transferring old photographs of family members to cloth.

Barb continues. "As a computer consultant, I knew what computers could do. I knew how to research to find the best equipment that would accomplish my goals. I dearly wanted to learn to manipulate images on the computer and then print them to fabric so I could continue quilting," she explains.

Barb purchased a printer capable of printing images on fabric to broaden her techniques for her art quilts. She also recognized that she could use this equipment to make extra money if she could find other people who wanted images transferred to fabric. She asked members of a quilter's e-mail list for their opinions about what type of items the public would like most. Their response convinced Barb that T-shirts designed and printed by computer would be popular. Always open to new ideas, Barb decided to try her hand designing and selling these on the Internet.

Barb began showing her work everywhere she went. Explains Barb, "Further research at two quilters' camps I attended proved that when customers could see my products with transferred photo images, I could sell even more.

"Internet networking with quilting friends I met online helped me establish further contacts. This, in turn, led to better sales through a popular quilters' catalog," says Barb. However, Barb's image transfer service was less profitable than she had hoped it would be, since it was a costly process and quite labor-intensive. Competition from commercial copy transfer companies challenged her.

Relying on her research skills again, Barb decided to compete by permitting customers to alter the images they wanted her to transfer. For example, she offered to simplify existing backgrounds, remove cracks from old photos and mix images in creative ways.

Barb admits she has not marketed her products as aggressively as possible because she recognizes her art quilts as her true passion. She wants to guard against her image printing business overtaking her dedication to her prime interest of making art quilts—a difficult balancing act.

The Internet brings Barb customers for her art quilts. She now aims to expand her image-to-fabric business so it will support her quilting, allowing her to make any quilt she imagines without worrying about costs. Meanwhile, she continues to explore the use of computer images on art quilts. "I've had success with my unique method, having my quilts accepted in several national shows, including the 1996 American Quilting Society show," she says with pride. Barb also won a recent award for another of her computer transfer art quilts in an All-American Quilt Contest sponsored by *Good Housekeeping* and the Coming Home division of Lands' End.

Barb's experience led her to integrate everything in her life with her quilting. She explains, "My scientific experience helps me approach problems and solutions in a systematic way." Barb advises others, "Find out what type of quilting appeals to you and structure your quilt-related business to your unique talents and interests."

BARBARA BARRICK MCKIE: GRAPHIC MEMORIES BY MCKIE
40 Bill Hill Road, Lyme, CT 06371-3501
Phone:
(860) 434-5222
E-mail:
GENEBARB@aol.com

CHAPTER TEN

RESOURCES

List of Quilt Magazines

AMERICAN PATCHWORK AND QUILTING
1912 Grand Avenue
Des Moines, IA 50309-3884

AMERICAN QUILTER
(published by the American Quilting Society)
P.O. Box 3290
Paducah, KY 42002-3290

ART QUILT MAGAZINE
P.O. Box 630927
Houston, TX 77263-0927

CREATIVE QUILTING MAGAZINE
950 Third Avenue
New York, NY 10022

LADY'S CIRCLE PATCHWORK QUILTS
4969 Lerch Drive
Shady Side, MD 20764

MCCALL'S QUILTING
405 Riverhills Business Park
Birmingham, AL 35242

MINIATURE QUILTS
Chitra Publications
2 Public Avenue
Montrose, PA 18801-1220

QUICK & EASY QUILTING
306 East Parr Road
Berne, IN 46711

QUILTER'S NEWSLETTER MAGAZINE
741 Corporate Circle, Suite A
Golden, CO 80401-5622

QUILTING INTERNATIONAL
243 Newton-Sparta Road
Newton, NJ 07860

QUILTING QUARTERLY
(published by the National Quilting Association)
P.O. Box 393
Ellicott City, MD 21041-0393

QUILTING TODAY
Chitra Publications
2 Public Avenue
Montrose, PA 18801-1220

QUILT MAGAZINE
1115 Broadway
New York, NY 10010

QUILTMAKER MAGAZINE
P.O. Box 4101
Golden, CO 80402-4101

QUILT WORLD
306 East Parr Road
Berne, IN 46711

SEW MANY QUILTS
by Liz Porter and Marianne Fons
P.O. Box 2262
Birmingham, AL 35201

TRADITIONAL QUILTWORKS
Chitra Publications
2 Public Avenue
Montrose, PA 18801-1220

TRADITIONAL QUILTER
243 Sparta-Newton Road
Newton, NJ 07860

Trade Journals

Craft & Needlework Age, P.O. Box 420, Englishtown, NJ 07726. Comprehensive trade journal for all crafts, including quilting.

Crafts Fair Guide, The, Lee Spiegel, P.O. Box 5508, Mill Valley, CA 94942. Lee provides the most comprehensive reviews of fairs across the U.S.

Craftrends/Sew Business, 6201 Howard Street, Niles, IL 60714. Trade journal covering needlework/fabric/sewing/quilting. Includes quarterly publication, *Quilt Quarterly*, within the *Sew Business* section of this magazine.

Crafts Report, The, P.O. Box 1992, Wilmington, DE 19899. Prestigious journal for serious artisans. Magazine covers business, legal aspects, advertising, photography, taxes and financial advice plus display supplies and listings of consignment shops, fairs, scholarships and workshops across the U.S.

Craft Supply Directory Magazine, P.O. Box 420, 225 Gordons Corner Road, Manalapan, NJ 07726. Trade magazine aimed at professional crafters seeking vendors.

Professional Quilter, The, Morna McEver Golletz, Editor, 104 Bramblewood Lane, Lewisberry, PA 17339. Journal covering all aspects of professional quilting.

Books, Newsletters and Magazines

Consulting

Holtz, Herman. *How to Succeed as an Independent Consultant.* New York, NY: Wiley Press, 1993.

Lant, Dr. Jeffrey. *The Consultant's Kit.* Cambridge, MA: JLA Publications, 1981.
———— *Tricks of the Trade.* Cambridge, MA: JLA Publications, 1986.

Copyright (Books)

Blue, Martha and Marion Davidson. *Making It Legal.* Flagstaff, AZ: Northland Publishing, 1988.

Copyright Law of the United States of America. The definitive handbook on copyright information. Published by the Library of Congress (see page 105 for address).

DuBoff, Leonard. *The Law in Plain English for Craftspeople.* Loveland, Colorado: Interweave Press, 1984, 1988, 1991, 1993.

Fishman, Stephen. *The Copyright Handbook.* Berkeley, CA: Nolo Press, 1992.

Young, Woody. *Copyright Law: What You Don't Know Can Cost You!* Fountain Valley, CA: Joy Publishing, 1989.

Copyright (Newsletter)

Dukelow, Ruth H. "What Every Quilter Needs to Know About Copyright." *Quilter's Newsletter,* July 1991.

Craft Business

Brabec, Barbara. *Creative Cash.* Barrington, IL: Countryside Books, 1979.
———— *Handmade for Profit.* New York: Evans Publishing, 1996.

Hawkins, Wes. "Space for a Quiltmaker." *American Quilter Magazine,* pp. 30-33, Winter 1994.

Heim, Judy. *The Needlecrafter's Computer Companion.* San Francisco, CA: No Starch Press, 1995.

Landman, Sylvia. *Crafting for Dollars: Turn Your Hobby Into Serious Cash.* Rocklin, CA: Prima Publishing, 1996.

Long, Steve and Cindy. *You Can Make Money From Your Arts and Crafts.* Scott's Valley, CA: Mark Publishing, 1988.

Palmer/Pletsch Associates. *Sewing Room Design.* Portland, OR.

General Business

Brabec, Barbara. *Homemade Money.* Cincinnati, OH: Betterway Books, 1995.

Brooks, Julie K. *How to Write a Successful Business Plan.* New York: AMA COM, 1987.

Edwards, Paul and Sarah. *Making It on Your Own.* Los Angeles: Jeremy Tarcher Publications, 1991.

———— *Working From Home.* Los Angeles: Jeremy Tarcher Publications, 1985.

Elias, Stephen and Marcia Stewart. *Simple Contracts for Personal Use.* Berkeley, CA: Nolo Press, 1991.

Ireland, Susan. *The Complete Idiot's Guide to the Perfect Resume,* New York: Alpha Books, 1996.

Interviewing

Brady, John. *The Craft of Interviewing.* New York: Vintage Books, 1977.

Schumacher, Michael. *The Writer's Complete Guide to Conducting Interviews.* Cincinnati, OH: Writer's Digest Books, 1993.

Mail Order

Catalog Business and Direct Marketing News, 19 W. 21st Street, New York, NY 10010. (Both newspapers give free subscriptions to qualified mail-order sellers.)

Kremer, John. *Mail Order Selling Made Easier.* Fairfield, IA: Ad-Lip Publications, 1983.

Simon, Julian. *How to Start and Operate a Mail-Order Business,* 5th edition. New York: McGraw-Hill, 1993.

Weckesser, Ernest. *Dollars in Your Mailbox.* Erie, PA: Green Tree Press, 1986.

Wilbur, L. Perry. *Money in Your Mailbox.* New York: Wiley Press, 1985.

Marketing

Brodsky, Bart and Janet Geis. *Finding Your Niche . . . Marketing Your Professional Service.* Berkeley, CA: Community Resource Institute Press, 1992.

Edwards, Paul and Sarah and Laura Clampitt Douglas. *Getting Business to Come to You.* Los Angeles: Jeremy Tarcher Publications, 1991.

Levinson, Jay Conrad. *Guerrilla Marketing.* Boston: Houghton Mifflin, 1993.

Smith, Brian R. *Successful Marketing for Small Business.* Lexington, MA: Lewis Publishing Co., 1984.

Public Speaking

Burgett, Gordon, and Mike Frank. *Speaking for Money.* Carpenteria, CA: Communications Unlimited, 1985.

Ott, John. *How to Write and Deliver a Speech.* New York: Rolls Offset Printing Co., 1976.

Quick, John. *A Short Book on the Subject of Speaking.* New York: Washington Square Press, 1978.

Vassallo, Wanda. *Speaking With Confidence.* Cincinnati, OH: Betterway Books, 1990.

Teaching

Brodsky, Bart, and Janet Geis. *The Teaching Marketplace.* Berkeley, CA: Community Resource Institute Press, 1992.

Margolis, Fredric and Chip Bell. *Instructing for Results.* San Diego: Lakewood Publications, 1986. (Though written for those presenting classes in the corporate workplace, this book offers a wealth of information about adult education, communication skills in a classroom situation, handling difficult students, how to answer questions and evaluating your classes.)

The Second Treasury of Techniques for Teaching Adults. Washington, DC: National Association for Public Continuing and Adult Education, 1973. (See page 154 for address listed under Organizations.)

A Treasury of Techniques for Teaching Adults. Washington, DC: National Association for Public Continuing and Adult Education, 1970.

Writing (Books)

Brohaugh, William. *Write Tight.* Cincinnati, OH: Writer's Digest Books, 1993. (The *best* book on creating professional, concise text.)

Burgett, Gordon. *Query Letters/Cover Letters . . . How They Sell Your Writing.* Carpenteria, CA: Communication Unlimited, 1985.

Cool, Lisa Collier. *How to Write Irresistible Query Letters.* Cincinnati, OH: Writer's Digest Books, 1987.

Dowis, Richard. *How to Make Your Writing Reader-Friendly.* Crozier, VA: Betterway Books, 1990.

Price, Jonathan. *Thirty Days to More Powerful Writing.* New York: Fawcett Columbine, 1981.

Ross-Larson, Bruce. *Edit Yourself.* New York: W.W. Norton, 1982.

Venolia, Jan. *Rewrite Right!* Berkeley, CA: Ten Speed Press, 1981.

Zinsser, William. *On Writing Well,* 4th ed. Cincinnati, OH: Writer's Digest Books, 1990.

Writing (Magazines)

Byline. P.O. Box 130596, Edmund, OK 73013

The Professional Writer. P.O. Box 7427, Berkeley, CA 94707

Writer's Digest. 1507 Dana Avenue, Cincinnati, OH 45207

Writer's Journal. P.O. Box 25376, St. Paul, MN 55125

The Writer. 120 Boylston Street, Boston, MA 02116-4615

Marketing Resources

Below is a list of public library resources to help you research your market.

The Cumulative Book Index lists books published on a specific subject.

Gale Directory of Newspapers and Periodicals lists magazines and newspapers printed in the U.S.

The Industrial Index lists article titles published in trade journals. Though such journals have limited readership, they are highly specialized and contain valuable information.

The *Standard Rate & Data Service* lists TV stations, radio, newspapers, magazines, trade and business publications alphabetically and by category. It also lists the owners' names, addresses, dates of publication, advertising rates, size and cost of advertising space and display ads, and deadlines.

The Thomas Register, formerly only in libraries, is now available on the World Wide Web at: http://www.thomasregister.com:8000.

Government Contacts

Federal Trade Commission, Division of Legal & Public Records, Washington, DC 20580. Request free booklet: *A Business Guide to the Federal Trade Commission's Mail-Order Rule*.

Internal Revenue Service: Call (800) 829-3676 and request a copy of their *Free Tax Publications*. When it arrives, check off all of the topics you find of interest and call the office again. Your free publications will be mailed to you. Also, check out the IRS World Wide Web site on the Internet. You can download copies of most of the IRS literature.

Library of Congress, U.S. Copyright Office, Washington, DC 20559. Request free list of free publications and books.

U.S. Patent & Trademark Office, Washington DC 20231. Request free booklets: *General Information Concerning Trademarks* and *Basic Facts About Trademarks*.

Organizations

American Quilter's Society, P.O. Box 3290, Paducah, KY 42002-3290. Supports the Museum of the American Quilter's Society in addition to providing conventions, events and awards for quilters. Dedicated to preserving the history of American quiltmaking. Offers membership and quarterly publication, *American Quilter.*

American Sewing Guild, P.O. Box 8568, Medford, OR 97504. (800) 325-1882. Sponsors seminars, workshops, demonstrations, fashion shows, vendor malls.

Association of Crafts & Creative Industries, 1100-H Brandywine Boulevard, P.O. Box 2188, Zanesville, OH 43702. Website: http//www.connect2.org/cc. Sponsors shows, awards, exhibits and conventions for the entire craft industry, including quilting.

Hobby Industry Association, 319 East 54th Street, P.O. Box 348, Elmwood, NJ 07407. See chapter eight for information about HIA services.

International Quilt Market & International Quilt Festival, 7660 Woodway, Suite 550, Houston, TX 77063, (713) 781-6864, extension #301; Fax (713) 781-8182.

National Association for Public Continuing & Adult Education, National Education Association, 1201 Sixteenth Street, N.W., Washington, DC 20036.

National Quilting Association, Inc. P.O. Box 393 Ellicott City, MD 21041-0393. NQA, the oldest national quilting organization, supports quilters in many ways including, quarterly publication, *Quilting Quarterly;* sponsoring annual quilt shows, exhibits and workshops; providing individual programs that include certification and special newsletters for quilting teachers and judges. Provides grants and scholarship awards. Also maintains the National Quilt Registry for quilts made since 1976.

Quilters' Network, Terri Nyman, 4967 Lerch Drive, Shady Side, MD 20764. Offers a comprehensive directory of available quilting teachers with descriptions of their workshops.

Society of Craft Designers, P.O. Box 2188, Zanesville, OH 43702-2188. See chapter nine for broad coverage of SCD.

Southeastern Fabrics, Notions & Crafts Assoc., Inc. P.O. Box 937, Duluth, GA 30136.

Catalogs

A to Z Designs, 13882 Montecito Drive, Victorville, CA 92392. (619) 243-4546. Specializes in dark and pastel fabrics for Amish quilting plus frames and Dazor lamps.

Books Unlimited from ASN Publishers, 1455 Linda Vista Drive, San Marcos, CA 92069. (619) 471-2320; Fax (619) 591-0230. Orders only: (800) 345-1752.

Clotilde, Sewing/Quilting Notions, 2 Sew Smart Way B8031, Stevens Point, WI 54481-8031. (800) 772-2891. (Always 20 percent discount.)

Connecting Threads For the Busy Quilter, P.O. Box 8940, Vancouver, WA 98668-8940. (800) 574-6454. General quilting products.

Contemporary Quilting, 173 Post Road, Fairfield, CT, 06430. (203) 259-3564. Specializes in fabric only.

Cotton Club, P.O. Box 2263, Boise, ID 83701. Fax (208) 345-1217. E-mail: cotton@micron.net. Website: http://www.cottonclub.com. More than a mail-order catalog for quality quilting fabrics, the Cotton Club offers regular fabric memberships which include special collections like sample watercolor packets. Full-sized four-inch squares are large enough to be included in quilts. Members may also buy books at 20 percent off list price.

Country Quilter, 344 Route 100, Somers, NY 10589. (914) 277-4820. Quilting pattern company featuring whimsical quilt designs.

Crazy Quilter's Club and Catalog, 69 Coolidge Avenue, Haverhill, MA 01832. (800) 666-3562. Specializing in patterns and supplies for crazy quilts.

Design Plus, 907 Columbia Road, Fort Collins, CO 80525. (970) 484-7055. Owner Heidi Wurst will mail color sheets and actual samples of custom-made quilt labels upon request. Makes and prints labels to include quiltmaker's name, address, phone number and other quilting details.

Dover Street Booksellers, 8673 Commerce Drive #13, P.O. Box 1563, Easton, MD 21601. (410) 822-9329. Orders only: (800) 235-5358. Comprehensive quilting book catalog.

EZ International Quilt Shop, 95 Mayhill Street, Saddle Brook, NJ 07662. (201) 712-1234; Fax: (201) 712-1199. Books, patterns, tools and notions. Specializes in plastic templates and rulers.

Flynn Quilt Frame Company, 1000 Shiloh Overpass Road, Billings, MT 59106. (800) 745-3596. Specializes in quilt frames, stands, tools, patterns and quilting books by John Flynn.

Gray Wind Publishing, 308 W. U.S. Hwy 34, Phillips, NE 68865. (402) 886-2281. Specializes in quilting books and patterns, including foundation paper-piecing patterns.

Hancock's, 3841 Hinkleville Road, Paducah, KY 42001. (800) 845-8723; Fax (502) 442-2164. Complete catalog of fabric, notions, batting, tools and books.

Home Craft Services, 340 W. 5th Street, Kansas, MO 64105. Offers pre-cut quilt pieces and kits.

House of White Birches Quilting Catalog, 306 East Parr Road, Berne, IN 46711. (800) 347-9887. Offers quilting patterns, books and general quilting supplies.

Keepsake Quilting, Route 25B, P.O. Box 1618, Centre Harbor, NH 03226-1618. Comprehensive catalog of patterns, books, notions and fabrics.

Kirk Collection, 1513 Military Avenue, Omaha, NE 68111. (402) 551-0386. E-mail: KirkColl@aol.com. Specializing in antique fabrics and quilts from 1850-1950 plus quality reproduction fabrics, wool and silk battings, books and notions.

Mace Motif, 106 Manito Road, Manasquan, NY 08736. (908) 223-4434. Catalog features rotary-cutting templates and stained glass quilting books and patterns.

M.C., 2852 Jeff Davis Highway, Suite 109, P.O. Box 11, Stafford, VA 22554. (703) 720-6758. Rotary turntables and mats.

Newport Quilt and Gift Co., 644 SW Coast Highway, Suite B, Newport, OR 97365. Offers watercolor flower blocks and fabric by mail.

Now & Then Publications, 725 Beach Street, Ashland, OR 97520. (541) 482-7935. Specializes in how-to-quilt books for children.

PBH Foundation Patterns, 1617 Ashby Avenue, Berkeley, CA 94703. (510) 843-3071. Wholesale and retail paper foundation patterns.

Patchwork, 6676 Amsterdam Road, Amsterdam, MT 59741. (406) 282-7218; Fax: (406) 282-7322. E-mail: ptchwrks@alpinet.net. Website: http//www.alpinet.net/~ptchwrks. Specializing in reproduction fabrics from 1775 to 1950.

Patchwork N' Things, P.O. Box 3725, Granada Hills, CA 91394. (818) 360-2828. Quilt supplies and notions.

Pieces of Dreams, P.O. Box 298, Running Springs, CA 92382. (909) 867-3764. Hand-painted and space-dyed fabrics.

PineTree Quilting: 585 Broadway, South Portland, ME, 04106. Large selection of natural fiber and poly batts; appliqué aids; fabric pencils and markers; templates and template plastic; needlecraft gloves; rotary cutters, clippers, snippers and scissors; machine sewing needles; seven brands of hand-sewing needles and threads. PineTree sells books at 20 percent off retail; e-mail the book title and author's name for a price quote. Check PineTree's catalog at http://quilt.com/Pinetree or e-mail your name and address to request the catalog. PineTree answers questions about quilting products at aardvark@ime.net.

Practical Patchwork, 123 West Third Street, Mountain View, MO 65548. Offers fabric kits and fabric.

Professional Quilter Publications, 104 Bramblewood Lane, Lewisberry, PA 17339. (717) 691-8176. Features books, leaflets and other career resources for professional quilters.

Quakertown Quilts, 607 Friendswood Drive, Friendswood, TX 77546. (713) 996-1756. Offers fabric, books, patterns, notions, classes and services. Wholesale inquiries welcome.

Quilt Broker Internet Service, 907 Columbia Road, Fort Collins, CO 80525. (970)

484-7055. Specializes in selling new and previously owned quilts, catering to interior designers and collectors.

Quilter's Bookshelf, 3244 N. Hackett Avenue, Milwaukee, WI 53211. (414) 332-2290; Fax (414) 332-2788. Comprehensive selection of quilt books.

Quilter's Catalog, 9015 Highway 40 NW, Montevideo, MN 56265. Orders Only: (800) 637-2541. Books, templates, patterns and tools from quilts shown on Sharlene Jorgenson's quilt program on PBS.

Quilter's Dream Enterprises, Suite 703, 15100 S.E. 38th Street, 101, Bellevue, WA 98006. Quilting books and tools discount catalog.

Quilter's Haven, P.O. Box 4873, Covina, CA 91723. (818) 339-4788. General quilting supplies.

Quilter's Resource, P.O. Box 148850, Chicago, IL 60614. (612) 793-6782; (800) 637-2541; Fax (312) 278-1348. Orders only. General quilting supplies.

Quilter's Rule International, 2322 N.E. 29th Avenue, Ocala, FL 34470. Orders only: (800) 343-8691; Fax: (904) 368-2289, (904) 368-9070. Wholesale quilting supplies.

Quilt Farm, P.O. Box 7877, Saint Paul, MN 55107. (612) 293-0204. Orders only: (800) 435-6201. Offers comprehensive array of tools, notions, fabrics, patterns and books.

Quilt House, 95 Mayhill Street, Saddle Brook, NJ 07663. (201) 712-1234; (800) 660-0415; Fax: (201) 712-1199. Website: http//www.ezquilt.com. Specializes in tools and templates.

Quilts & Other Comforts, 1 Quilters Lane, P.O. Box 4100, Golden, CO 80401. Fax: (303) 277-0370. Orders only: (800) 881-6624. Offers comprehensive catalog of books, patterns, tools and notions.

QuiltSmith, LTD, 252 Cedar Road, Poquoson, VA 23662. Precision metal, nonskid quilting templates made by ARDCO ™.

Quiltwork Patches, 209 SW 2nd Street, P.O. Box 724, Corvallis, OR 97339. General quilting supplies.

Quiltworks, 1055 E. 79th Street, Minneapolis, MN 55420. (612) 854-1460; (800) 328-1850; Fax: (612) 854-7254. Comprehensive catalog of books, patterns and fabrics.

Schoolhouse Enterprises, P.O. Box 305, Tuckahoe, NJ 08250-0305. Voice mail: (609) 628-2256. Exclusive manufacturers of Gridded Geese products.

Stencils and Stuff, 5198 TR 123, Millersburg, OH 44654. Stencils, thread, notions.

Skydyes, 83 Richmond Lane, West Hartford, CT 06711. (203) 232-1429. Hand-painted cotton and silk fabrics.

Publishers of Quilt Books

ASN Publishing, Creative Ideas for Quilters, 1455 Linda Vista Drive, San Marcos, CA 92069. (800) 379-9627.

C & T Publishing, P.O. Box 1456, Lafayette, CA 94549. (800) 284-1114.

That Patchwork Place Inc., P.O. Box 118, Bothell, WA 98041-0118. (800) 426-3126; Fax: (206) 486-7596. E-mail: info@patchwork.com. Website: http//oak.forest.net/patchwork.

Quilt Digest Press, 4255 West Tougy Avenue, Lincolnwood, IL 60646-1975. (800) 323-4900.

Quilting Software

Electric Quilt. The Electric Quilt Co., 1039 Melrose Street, Bowling Green, OH 43402. Orders only: (800) 356-4219. Technical support: (419) 352-1134. E-mail: aquiltco@wcnet.org.

PC Quilt. Designer Nina Antze designed this program first for IBM/DOS and later developed a version for Macintosh users called Baby Mac. Nina Antze, 7061 Lynch Road, Sebastopol, CA 95472. E-mail: NinaA@aol.com.

Quilter's Design Studio. Windows & Macintosh, P.O. Box 19946, San Diego, CA 92159-0946.

Quilt-Pro. Windows drawing program to create quilts. Call (800) 884-1511 for a free demo disk and ordering information.

QuiltSoft. Windows drawing program. P.O. Box 19946, San Diego, CA 92159-0946. (619) 583-2970; Fax: (619) 583-2682.

Vquilt 2. P.O. Box 129, Jarrettsville, MD 21084. (410) 557-6871.

Quilt-Related World Wide Web Sites

AlphaMall Shopping http://alphamall.qc.ca. Bulletin board for free ads, directory of quilt shops.

American Crafters for Professional Crafters http://www.ProCrafter.com.

American Craft Malls http://www.procrafter.com/procraft.

A Stitch in Time http://www.cloudnet.com/~astitch. News about dolls, quilts, sewing.

C & T Publishing http://www.ctpub.com. Quilting book publisher.

Coomer's Malls http://www.coomers.com. Philip Coomer, founder of Coomer's Craft Malls in shopping malls across the U.S., offers his craft bulletin board.

CraftNet Village http://www.craftet.org. Opportunities and newsletter for all crafters.

Craft Supply Magazine http://www.craftsupply.com. E-mail: Silkee@internexus.net.

CraftWeb http://www.craftweb.com. Opportunities and newsletter for all crafters.

David Walker's Quilting Website http://w3.one.net/~davidxix.

Gallery of Textile Works http://www.penny-nii.com. Quilt gallery on the Web.

High Tech Quilting http://www.infinet.com:80/~jan. Jan Cabral's collection of digital fabrics and related computer quilt drawing techniques.

Hobby Industry Association http://www.webcreations.com.

Mary-Jo McCarthy's Southwest Decoratives http://www.cyspacemalls.com/quilt. 191 Big Horn Ridge NE, Albuquerque, NM 87122. (505) 856-7254; Fax: (505) 856-7270. E-mail: MjoMc@aol.com. Request catalog by name, "Make It Southwest Style." (See chapter three for more information.)

National Patchwork Association http://www.paston.co.uk/natpat/natpat. E-mail: trinity@paston.co.uk United Kingdom. Lists quilt shops and quilting events in the U.K.

Needlecrafter's Computer Companion. Judy Heim, author. http://www.execpc.com/~judyheim. Tips from Judy's book and columns about craft-related computer software.

Nine Patch News http://www.members.aol.com/ninepatchn/index.html. Home page for Quilt Forum on America Online.

Professional Crafter http://www.procrafter.com. A marketplace for all crafts, including quilts. Will advertise your products for a monthly fee and will create websites.

QuiltArt http://www.quilt.net. E-mail: quiltart.digest@lists.his.com. An Internet quiltsite and mailing list for contemporary art quilters.

Quilter's Corner http://www.qcx.com. Julie Higgins' website. (See chapter one for more information.)

Quilting From the Heartland http://www.qheartland.com. TV quilter Sharlene Jorgensen's website.

Quilt Magazine http://www.quilt.net/quiltmag. Related articles from the magazine.

Textile Information Management System http://www.unicate.com//Timsfaq.html. E-mail: uni@unicate.com. Canadian-based service providing interactive system for lining textile, apparel and fashion industry. Members can buy, sell, display and advertise.

Virtual Quilt http://www.tvq.com. Excellent online newsletter plus mail order for fabrics, antique quilts and patterns. Reviews quilting software.

World Wide Quilt Page http://www.tvq.com. Offers patterns, guild listings, book reviews, galleries, teacher listing and block exchanges.

Yahoo's Quilting Events http://yahoo.com/Arts/Textiles/Quilting/Events. Many quilting links and websites.

Online Quilt Groups

Contact the following online chat groups by e-mail. All are interactive and international quilt groups open to all quilters.

Interquilt mbishop@needles.com

Kaffeel-Klatsch E-mail: kaffeel-klatsch@quilt.com

Quilt Art quiltart@quilt.net

QuiltBee quiltbee@quilter.com

Quilt Biz ozzg@nmia.com

See also the comprehensive list of online groups and services, including those sponsored by specific vendors—such as America Online, CompuServe and so on—in the article, "Your Computer Quilting Neighborhood," by Betty Roved and Jim Burchell, *Quilter's Newsletter Magazine,* April 1996 issue.

Commercial vendors providing online services:

America Online: (800) 827-6364

CompuServe: (800) 487-0588

Delphi: (800) 695-4005

Genie: (800) 638-9636

Prodigy: (800) PRODIGY

Index

More Great Books for Crafters!

How to Show & Sell Your Crafts—Turn your craft show sales into a profitable business! You'll learn how to display your products in the best possible way, increase sales through improved marketing and salesmanship, and expand your business by exploring the many outlets for showing and selling your crafts. #70374/$18.99/160 pages/92 b&w illus./paperback

How to Make Enchanting Miniature Teddy Bears—Create adorable little bears with fuzzy fabric, a snippet of thread, and the step-by-step instructions you'll find in this handy reference. Ten illustrated projects take you through a range of projects—from a simple teddy bear pin to a range of teddies with different styles and moveable limbs. #30846/$22.99/128 pages/212 color illus./paperback

Easy Airbrush Projects for Crafters & Decorative Painters—Using the airbrush for crafts and decorative painting has never been easier! You'll get the inside story on getting started in airbrushing and basic painting techniques. Then, move on to 10 step-by-step projects that perfect what you've learned. #30908/$23.99/128 pages/356 color, 18 b&w illus./paperback

Creating Extraordinary Beads From Ordinary Materials—Transform run-of-the-mill materials into uncommonly beautiful beads! No experience or fancy equipment is required—just follow 53 step-by-step projects to get great results using everyday materials like construction paper, fabric scraps, yarn and more! #30905/$22.99/128 pages/326 color, 18 b&w illus./paperback

The Crafter's Guide to Pricing Your Work—Price and sell more than 75 kinds of crafts with this must-have reference. You'll learn how to set prices to maximize income while maintaining a fair profit margin. Includes tips on record-keeping, consignment selling, taxes, reducing costs and managing your cash flow. #70353/$16.99/160 pages/paperback

How to Start Making Money With Your Crafts—Launch a rewarding crafts business with this guide that starts with the basics—from creating marketable products to setting the right prices—and explores all the exciting possibilities. End-of-chapter quizzes, worksheets, ideas and lessons learned by successful crafters are included to increase your learning curve. #70302/$18.99/176 pages/35 b&w illus./paperback

Selling Your Dolls and Teddy Bears—Earn as you learn the business, public relations and legal aspects of doll and teddy bear sales. Some of the most successful artists in the business share the nitty-gritty details of pricing, photographing, tax planning, customer relations and more! #70352/$18.99/160 pages/31 b&w illus./paperback

Painting & Decorating Birdhouses—Turn unfinished birdhouses into something special—from a quaint Victorian roost to a Southwest pueblo, from a rustic log cabin to a lighthouse! These colorful and easy decorative painting projects are for the birds with 22 clever projects to create indoor decorative birdhouses, as well as functional ones to grace your garden. #30882/$23.99/128 pages/194 color illus./paperback

The Best of Silk Painting—Discover inspiration in sophisticated silk with this gallery of free-flowing creativity. Over 100 full-color photos capture the glorious colors, unusual textures and unique designs of 77 talented artists. #30840/$29.99/128 pages/136 color illus.

Painting Houses, Cottages and Towns on Rocks—Turn ordinary rocks into charming cottages, country churches and Victorian mansions! Accomplished artist Lin Wellford shares 11 fun, inexpensive, step-by-step projects that are sure to please. #30823/$21.99/128 pages/398 color illus./paperback

Making Greeting Cards With Rubber Stamps—Discover hundreds of quick, creative, stamp-happy ways to make extra-special cards—no experience, fancy equipment or expensive materials required! You'll find 30 easy-to-follow projects for holidays, birthdays, thank you's and more! #30821/$21.99/128 pages/231 color illus./paperback

Acrylic Decorative Painting Techniques—Discover stroke-by-stroke instruction that takes you through the basics and beyond! More than 50 fun and easy painting techniques are illustrated in simple demonstrations that offer at least 2 variations on each method. Plus, a thorough discussion on tools, materials, color, preparation and backgrounds. #30884/$24.99/128 pages/550 color illus.

How to Make Clay Characters—Bring cheery clay characters to life! The creator of collectible clay "Pippsywoggins" figures shares her fun and easy techniques for making adorable little figures—no sculpting experience required! #30881/$22.99/128 pages/579 color illus./paperback

Decorative Painting Sourcebook—Priscilla Hauser, Phillip Myer and Jackie Shaw lend their expertise to this one-of-a-kind guide straight from the pages of Decorative Artist's Workbook! You'll find step-by-step, illustrated instructions on every technique—from basic brushstrokes to faux finishes, painting glassware, wood, clothing and much more! #30883/$24.99/128 pages/200 color illus./paperback

Making Books by Hand—Discover 12 beautiful projects for making handmade albums, scrapbooks, journals and more. Only everyday items like cardboard, wrapping paper and ribbon are needed to make these exquisite books for family and friends. #30942/$24.99/108 pages/250 color illus.

Make It With Paper Series—Discover loads of bright ideas and easy-to-do projects for making colorful paper creations. Includes paper to cut and fold, templates and step-by-step instructions for designing your own creations. Plus, each paperback book has over 200 color illustrations to lead you along the way.

    Paper Boxes—#30935/$19.99/114 pages
    Paper Pop-Ups—#30936/$19.99/96 pages

The Decorative Stamping Sourcebook—Embellish walls, furniture, fabric and accessories—with stamped designs! You'll find 180 original, traceable motifs in a range of themes and illustrated instructions for making your own stamps to enhance any decorating style. #30898/$24.99/128 pages/200 color illus.

Make Jewelry Series—With basic materials and a little creativity you can make great-looking jewelry! Each 96-page paperback book contains 15 imaginative projects using materials from clay to fabric to paper—and over 200 color illustrations to make jewelry creation a snap!

    Make Bracelets—#30939/$15.99
    Make Earrings—#30940/$15.99
    Make Necklaces—#30941/$15.99

Handmade Jewelry: Simple Steps to Creating Wearable Art—Create unique and wearable pieces of art—and have fun doing it! 42 step-by-step jewelry-making projects are at your fingertips—from necklaces and earrings, to pins and barrettes. Plus, no experience, no fancy equipment and no expensive materials are required! #30820/$21.99/128 pages/126 color, 30 b&w illus./paperback

The Crafts Supply Sourcebook: A Comprehensive Shop-by-Mail Guide, 4th Edition—Turn here to find the materials you need—from specialty tools and the hardest-to-find accessories, to clays, doll parts, patterns, quilting machines and hundreds of other items! Listings organized by area of interest make it quick and easy! #70344/$18.99/320 pages/paperback

Master Strokes—Master the techniques of decorative painting with this comprehensive guide! Learn to use decorative paint finishes on everything from small objects and furniture to walls and floors, including dozens of step-by-step demonstrations and numerous techniques. #30937/$22.99/160 pages/400 color illus./paperback

The Doll Sourcebook—Bring your dolls and supplies as close as the telephone with this unique sourcebook of retailers, artists, restorers, appraisers and more! Each listing contains extensive information—from addresses and phone numbers to business hours and product lines. #70325/$22.99/352 pages/176 b&w illus./paperback

The Art of Painting Animals on Rocks—Discover how a dash of paint can turn humble stones into charming "pet rocks." This hands-on, easy-to-follow book offers a menagerie of fun—and potentially profitable—stone animal projects. Eleven examples, complete with materials lists, photos of the finished piece and patterns will help you create a forest of fawns, rabbits, foxes and other adorable critters. #30606/$21.99/144 pages/250 color illus./paperback

The Complete Flower Arranging Book—An attractive, up-to-date guide to creating more than 100 beautiful arrangements with fresh and dried flowers, illustrated with step-by-step demonstrations. #30405/$24.95/192 pages/300+ color illus.

The Teddy Bear Sourcebook: For Collectors and Artists—Discover the most complete treasury of bear information stuffed between covers. You'll turn here whenever you need to find sellers of bear making supplies, major manufacturers of teddy bears, teddy bear shows, auctions and contests, museums that house teddy bear collections and much more. #70294/$18.99/356 pages/202 illus./paperback

Priscilla Hauser's Book of Decorative Painting—Now you can learn to paint Priscilla Hauser's trademark roses—as well as daisies, lilacs, violets, tulips and other beautiful blooms! Over 20 step-by-step flower painting projects will give you endless ideas for using painted flowers to decorate a variety of surfaces. #30914/$24.99/144 pages/371 color, 22 b&w illus./paperback

Painting Flowers in Watercolor With Louise Jackson—Master decorative artist, Louise Jackson, shows you how to beautifully render one of decorative painting's most popular subjects—flowers! All you need is the desire to follow 15 detailed, step-by-step projects from start to finish! #30913/$23.99/128 pages/165 color, 21 b&w illus./paperback

Creative Finishes Series—Explore the world of creative finishing with leading decorative artist, Phil Myer! Each book features a variety of techniques, paint applications and surface treatments in 15 projects complete with detailed instructions, patterns and step-by-step photos.

    Painting & Decorating Tables—#30910/$23.99/112 pages/177 color illus./paperback
    Painting & Decorating Boxes—#30911/$23.99/112 pages/145 color, 32 b&w illus./paperback

Stencil Source Book 2—Add color and excitement to fabrics, furniture, walls and more with over 200 original motifs that can be used again and again! Idea-packed chapters will help you create dramatic color schemes and themes to enhance your home in hundreds of ways. #30730/$22.99/144 pages/300 illus.

The Complete Book of Silk Painting—Create fabulous fabric art—everything from clothing to pillows to wall hangings. You'll learn every aspect of silk painting in this step-by-step guide, including setting up a workspace, necessary materials and fabrics and specific silk painting techniques. #30362/$26.99/128 pages/color throughout

Fabric Sculpture: The Step-by-Step Guide & Showcase—Discover how to transform fabrics into 3-dimensional images. Seven professional fabric sculptors demonstrate projects that illustrate their unique approaches and methods for creating images from fabric. The techniques—covered in easy, step-by-step illustration and instruction—include quilting, thread work, applique and soft sculpture. #30687/$29.99/160 pages/300+ color illus.

Decorative Boxes To Create, Give and Keep—Craft beautiful boxes using techniques including embroidery, stenciling, lacquering, gilding, shellwork, decoupage and many others. Step-by-step instructions and photographs detail every project. #30638/$15.95/128 pages/color throughout/paperback

Elegant Ribboncraft—Over 40 ideas for exquisite ribbon-craft—hand-tied bows, floral garlands, ribbon embroidery and more. Various techniques are employed—including folding, pleating, plaiting, weaving, embroidery, patchwork, quilting, applique and découpage. All projects are complete with step-by-step instructions and photographs. #30697/$16.99/128 pages/130+ color illus./paperback

Nature Craft—Dozens of step-by-step nature craft projects to create, including dried flower garlands, baskets, corn dollies, potpourri and more. Bring the outdoors inside with these wonderful projects crafted with readily available natural materials. #30531/$16.99/144 pages/200 color illus./paperback

Paper Craft—Dozens of step-by-step paper craft projects to make, including greeting cards, boxes and desk sets, jewelry and pleated paper blinds. If you have ever worked with or wanted to work with paper you'll enjoy these attractive, fun-to-make projects. #30530/$16.95/144 pages/200 color illus./paperback

Everything You Ever Wanted to Know About Fabric Painting—Discover how to create beautiful fabrics! You'll learn how to set up work space, choose materials, plus the ins and outs of tie-dye, screen printing, woodgraining, marbling, cyanotype and more! #30625/$21.99/128 pages/color throughout/paperback

Gretchen Cagle's Decorative Painting Keepsakes—Discover a treasury of beautiful projects collected from one of today's most celebrated decorative painters! In her latest book, Gretchen shares 31 of her all-time favorite projects. No matter what your skill level, clear instructions, traceable patterns and color mixing recipes will have you painting in no time! #30975/$24.99/144 pages/91 color, 44 b&w illus./paperback

1,200 Paint Effects for the Home Decorator—Now you can find the ideal color combination and paint effect for any kind of job! This handy visual guide gives you over 1,200 combinations, based on 25 standard colors. Plus, step-by-step instructions for special finishing effects such as splattering, combing, color washing, marbling, distressing and more! #30949/$29.99/192 pages/1,000+ color illus.

Decorative Painting: Fruits, Vegetables and Berries—Create a cornucopia of projects with this guide to the secrets of painting luscious fruits, vegetables and berries! Over 40 popular subjects are demonstrated in easy-to-follow detail—including tips on equipment, color theory and preparation. #30904/$22.99/128 pages/300+ color illus./paperback

Create Your Own Greeting Cards and Gift Wrap With Priscilla Hauser—You'll see sponge prints, eraser prints, cellophane scrunching, marbleizing, papermaking and dozens of other techniques you can use to make unique greetings for all your loved ones. #30621/$24.99/128 pages/230 color illus.

Creative Paint Finishes for Furniture—Revive your furniture with fresh color and design! Inexpensive, easy and fun painting techniques are at your fingertips, along with step-by-step directions and a photo gallery of imaginative applications for faux finishing, staining, stenciling, mosaic, découpage and many other techniques. #30748/$27.99/144 pages/236 color, 7 b&w illus.

Master Works: How to Use Paint Finishes to Transform Your Surroundings—Discover how to use creative paint finishes to enhance and excite the "total look" of your home. This step-by-step guide contains dozens of exciting ideas on fresco, marbling, paneling and other simple paint techniques for bringing new life to any space. Plus, you'll also find innovative uses for fabrics, screens and blinds. #30626/$29.95/176 pages/150 color illus.

Creative Paint Finishes for the Home—A complete, full-color, step-by-step guide to decorating floors, walls and furniture—including how to use the tools, master the techniques and develop ideas. #30426/$27.99/144 pages/212 color illus.

Paint Craft—Discover great ideas for enhancing your home, wardrobe and personal items. You'll see how to master the basics of mixing and planning colors, how to print with screen and linoleum to create your own stationery, how to enhance old glassware and pottery pieces with unique patterns and motifs and much more! #30678/$16.95/144 pages/200 color illus./paperback

Fake Your Own Antiques—Transform junk-shop finds and ordinary furniture into eye-catching "antiques." Over 40 step-by-step projects include instructions for antiquing, distressing and creating patina on wood, metal, paper and other surfaces. #30841/$24.99/128 pages/200 illus.

100 Keys to Great Fabric Painting—Get 100 simple gems of advice from experienced fabric painters! You'll learn how to achieve professional results in a variety of techniques—including wax resist, beading and block printing. #30822/$17.99/64 pages/130 illus.

Making & Decorating Picture Frames—Create picture-perfect frames with these 45 imaginative and original projects using a variety of techniques. You'll work with several different materials—from paint and tin to paper and fabric—while discovering tips on choosing the right frame styles and colors to suit your picture. #30807/$24.99/128 pages/250 illus.